NS

GALLERY BOOKS
A DIVISION OF SIMON & SCHUSTER, INC.
1230 AVENUE OF THE AMERICAS
NEW YORK, NY 10020

FIRST MTV BOOKS/GALLERY BOOKS TRADE PAPERBACK EDITION OCTOBER 2010

GALLERY BOOKS AND COLOPHON ARE REGISTERED TRADEMARKS OF SIMON & SCHUSTER, INC.

FOR INFORMATION ABOUT SPECIAL DISCOUNTS FOR BULK PURCHASES, PLEASE CONTACT SIMON & SCHUSTER SPECIAL SALES AT
1-866-506-1949 OR BUSINESS@SIMONANDSCHUSTER.COM

THE SIMON & SCHUSTER SPEAKERS BUREAU CAN BRING AUTHORS TO YOUR LIVE EVENT. FOR MORE INFORMATION OR
TO BOOK AN EVENT CONTACT THE SIMON & SCHUSTER SPEAKERS BUREAU AT 1-866-248-3049 OR VISIT OUR WEBSITE AT
WWW.SIMONSPEAKERS.COM.

LAYOUT BY WALEIN DESIGN
ART PHOTOGRAPHED BY MATTHEW MACDONALD AND WALTER EINENKEL
RYAN GEE PHOTOGRAPHY: PAGES 22-23, 46-47, 70-71, 184-185, 218-219, 248-249, 270-271
ADAM WALLACAVAGE PHOTOGRAPHY: PAGES 34-35, 102-103, 286-287
ADDITIONAL PHOTOGRAPHY: ROGER BAGLEY, REDMOWHAWK GEOFF, JOE DEVITO, MARK WEISS,
CLAY PATRICK, JEFF TAYLOR, BAM & MISSY MARGERA

MANUFACTURED IN THE UNITED STATES OF AMERICA
FIRST EDITION
10  9  8  7  6  5  4  3  2  1

ISBN 978-1-4391-4773-3
ISBN 978-1-4391-4774-0 (PBK)

# SERIOUS AS DOG DIRT!

**GALLERY BOOKS**

Kenosha Public Library
Kenosha, WI

**MTV BOOKS**

**NEW YORK    LONDON    TORONTO    SYDNEY**

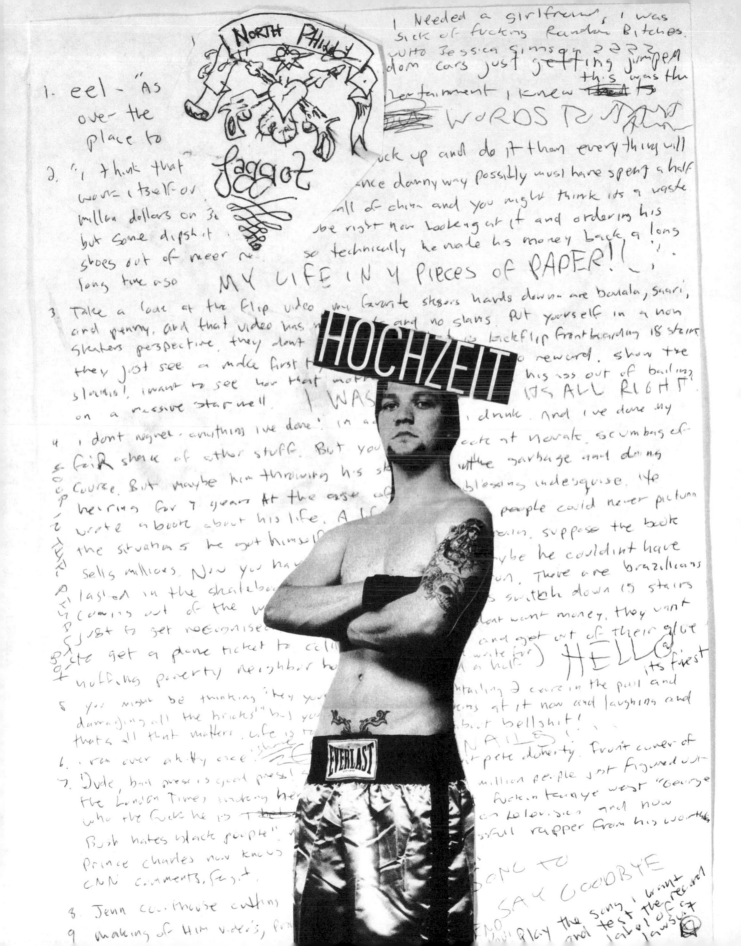

1. eel - "As over the place to

2. "I think that wore itself or... million dollars on 3... but some dipshit... shoes out of meer n... long time ago

North Philly — faggot

3 Take a look at the flip video my favorite skaters hands down are barala, saari, and penny, and that video was ... skaters perspective, they dont ... they just see a mdca first t... slomis! I want to see how that motr... on a massive stairwell. I WAS...

4 I dont regret anything I've done! in a...
5 fair share of other stuff. But you...
6 Course. But maybe him throwing his st...
  hearins for 7 years At the ease of...
  wrote a book about his life. A l...
  the situations he got himself...
  sells millions. Now you hav...
  lasted in the skateboa...
  comins out of the w...
  Just to get recognised...
  ...ste get a plane ticket to cell...
  nothing poverty neighbor ho...

5 you might be thinking "hey you...
  damaging all the tricks" but yo...
  thats all that matters. Life is ...

6. Ran over a kitty once...
7. Dude, bad press is good press!...
  the London Times making her...
  who the fuck he is T...
  Bush hates black people"...
  Prince charles now knows...
  CNN comments, fast...

8 Jenn courthouse cutting...
9 making of Him video's, fra...

I Needed a girlfriend, I was sick of fucking Random Bitches. who Jessica Simpson ???? dom cars just getting jumped this was th...
...ertainment I knew to WORDS TO ...

...uck up and do it than every thing will ...nce danny way possibly must have spent a half ...all of chim and you might think its a waste ...be right now looking at it and ordering his so technically he made his money back a long

MY LIFE IN 4 PIECES OF PAPER!!

...s and no stairs. Put yourself in a non ...kickflip front boarding 18 stairs ...o reward. show the ...his ass out of bailing ITS ALL RIGHT!

HOCHZEIT

...I drunk. And I've done my ...ects at novak scumbag ef ...the garbage and doing ...blessins in desquise. He ...people could never picturin ...suppose the book ...maybe he couldnt have ...un. There are brazillians ...switch down 15 stairs ...that want money. they want ...and get out of their glue (...write for) HELLO ...its first ...htailing 2 cars in the pool and ...ns at it now and laughing and ...about bellshit! NAILS!! ...t pete doherty. front cover of ...million people just figured out ...fuckin tanye west 'cause ...on television and now ...ssful rapper from his wort...

...ONE TO SAY GOODBYE ...the song I wrote ...and test the record label of 57 lawsuit

**Margera takes a break** from producing a video for his brother's bar

# Making the leap

m Margera, 21, of Chester County, has made a comfo

**By Robert Moran**
INQUIRER STAFF WRITER

Let's go to the tape: Bam Margera, 21, is about to leap off a Wilmington-area bridge into a river 50 feet below. Taking a page from the Wile E. Coyote book of famous stunts, he is holding an open picnic umbrella.

Of course, he drops like a stone, screaming an expletive as he tilts forward into an unintended belly flop.

"I was hoping to float like Mary Poppins," Margera concedes ruefully, "but it didn't work out so well."

MTV's *Jackass*, the any
of stupid-human tricks

But it more than pay
era, a high school dro
enough from skating
drive a black 1996 Aud
Audi S4, and to cough
payment recently for
wooded enclave not fa
hometown just outside

His success is testin
popularity and influen
now a $900 million bus

KY, to practice his skateboarding skills.

# to fame

## ble living off skateboarding.

-goes cavalcade
utter wit.

bills for Marg-
who now earns
dorsements to
and a blue 2000
$100,000 down
ew house in a
m his childhood
st Chester.

to the growing
f skateboarding,
s and the anchor
which start next

**Margera** is a s

BAM AT STOCKWELL

# JANUARY 1997

| SUNDAY | MONDAY | TUESDAY | WEDNESDAY | THURSDAY | FRIDAY | SATURDAY |
|---|---|---|---|---|---|---|
| **DECEMBER** 1 2 3 4 5 6 7 / 8 9 10 11 12 13 14 / 15 16 17 18 19 20 21 / 22 23 24 25 26 27 28 | **FEBRUARY** 1 / 2 3 4 5 6 7 8 / 9 10 11 12 13 14 15 / 16 17 18 19 20 21 22 / 23 24 25 26 27 28 | Jack Langeto | **1** snowboarded camelback  New Year's Day | **2** skated launch ramp wit Mike, DAY, MARI went to day's with kooz  NEW MOON | **3** went to foggoty Sand w/ Lenette and olivia  megans | **4** WOKE UP early Bombed the hill with Digity, Mic, Bird, ty, sue, mary irene wentoutback Birds bday tith vegas, lunatics, devings, clerans |
| **MEN?** | | **7** Stockwell Skatepark | **8** RADLANDS (NORTH HAMPTON) | **9** Fuck | **10** Southbank and London (photos w/ wig) | **11** London photos w/ wig |
| LONDON → | | | | | | |
| **13** went to Bristol w/ Danny | **14** | **15** | **16** | **17** Harrow + Stockwell | **18** | |
| **19** Liverpool | **20** Liverpool Birthday (Observed) | **21** | **22** | **23** LONDON photos w/ Daniel | **24** Glen G Gallery | **25** Stockwell Skatepark |
| **26** Stockwell Skatepark, meanwhile 2, and cantaloupes | **27** skated London photos w/ wig | **28** Stockwell photos w/ wig | **29** Radlands | **30** Left | **31** hung out w/ coxcutter |  This sentence has been placed here for no apparent reason |

LONDON

Bob Dole LIKES ousi MEN

# FEBRUARY

New

Roberckson
(302) 9 ...
Colleen ...
Zach bower (213) 7...
PHOTOGRAPHERS →

## 1997

| SUNDAY | MONDAY | TUESDAY | WEDNESDAY | THURSDAY | FRIDAY | SATURDAY |
|---|---|---|---|---|---|---|

**JANUARY**

|  |  |  | 1 | 2 | 3 | 4 |
|---|---|---|---|---|---|---|
| 5 | 6 | 7 | 8 | 9 | 10 | 11 |
| 12 | 13 | 14 | 15 | 16 | 17 | 18 |
| 19 | 20 | 21 | 22 | 23 | 24 | 25 |
| 26 | 27 | 28 | 29 | 30 | 31 |  |

**MARCH**

|  |  |  |  |  |  | 1 |
|---|---|---|---|---|---|---|
| 2 | 3 | 4 | 5 | 6 | 7 | 8 |
| 9 | 10 | 11 | 12 | 13 | 14 | 15 |
| 16 | 17 | 18 | 19 | 20 | 21 | 22 |
| 23 | 24 | 25 | 26 | 27 | 28 | 29 |
| 30 | 31 |  |  |  |  |  |

Ryan Gee (315) ...
dan wolfe ...
wallacavage (2...) ...
roberckson 302 ...
mick vocovich 619 ...
kelly vyan 2 ...
wig 0973 7 ...
... 619 ...
sturt 619 7 ...
kula 619 ...

**1** Shred For Life

**2** hung out w/chris, Hanna, phil did 101 sit ups gee + menser, mike joe, reab, matt stepen homade pizza on practice  
Groundhog Day

**3** went to DOE → Make, cantaloe ryan don go...

**4** went to east visited brandon watched mallrats w/ chris, mark and Jess went to bookstore wrote parts of a film w/ chris
OIL PLAYED, WATCHED MALLRATS

**5** went to mall w/ brandon wrote more of the FILM w/chris H.

**6** went to reading w/ mark, chris + phil skated MAGIC brandon camerower wrote more of the movie / went to wc diner

**7** NEW MOON went to glass co, produce junction, dollar store, home, dry ice, picked up raab, went home burger king UNDERGROUND PARTY w/oil went to dannys

**8** Filmed at ARTS

**9** went up chris/rade roberickson came over w/ Joe filmed scientist bran at arts went home to chill back to arts Jonel, Lisa

**10** mikes, burger king with Jeron, bran and chris went to Joes ground reward

**11** fairmans, Quarry, arts, movie place watched kids w/ brand + chris
Mardi Gras

**12** got TM package skated at east w/ mark bran Jess dug treasure at drive in w/chris **40**
Ash Wednesday Lincoln's Birthday

**13**

**14** St. Valentine's Day

**15** HEY YOU the reader FUCK YOU chilled w/ ART

**16** Filmed Coach bam and Rad scenes w/ Joe + Mike went to arts w/ keez

**17** Brandons Stand up Washington's Birthday (Observed) President's Day

**18** mike + merry left for cali brandon stayed over skated with blain hung out at Fairmon brandon Joes, deron Scattergories

**19** Skated w/ Jayson went over home with bran crys WCD

**20** Skated w/ Geoff Skated w/ Brian Scrimke

**21** Off Reading w/ Shrimka Skated w/ Geoff picked up chris went to tash + days drive around w/chris

**22** FULL MOON Quarry brandon hung out w/ chris + moore Washington's Birthday

**23** fairmans, Starweather Fairmore ... Lonestar brandon + eggs deron - Jess recording

**24** Joes CALIFORNIA

**25** Los Alamos GIANT MINI RAMP (filmed w/ SATVA) CALIFORNIA

**26** Birdhouse House skated w/ summer CALIFORNIA

**27** Shot cover drop in w/sturt CALIFORNIA

**28** skated HB CALIFORNIA

*OUTHOUSES*

717 6 ... seber

# MARCH  1997

| SUNDAY | MONDAY | TUESDAY | WEDNESDAY | THURSDAY | FRIDAY | SATURDAY |
|---|---|---|---|---|---|---|

| FEBRUARY / APRIL | | DREW | MAKE | CANTALOE | SCOTT | 1 Skated LA w/ Barley |
|---|---|---|---|---|---|---|

**FEBRUARY**
|  |  |  |  |  |  | 1 |
| 2 | 3 | 4 | 5 | 6 | 7 | 8 |
| 9 | 10 | 11 | 12 | 13 | 14 | 15 |
| 16 | 17 | 18 | 19 | 20 | 21 | 22 |
| 23 | 24 | 25 | 26 | 27 | 28 |  |

**APRIL**
|  |  | 1 | 2 | 3 | 4 | 5 |
| 6 | 7 | 8 | 9 | 10 | 11 | 12 |
| 13 | 14 | 15 | 16 | 17 | 18 | 19 |
| 20 | 21 | 22 | 23 | 24 | 25 | 26 |
| 27 | 28 | 29 | 30 |  |  |  |

CALIFORNIA

| 2 Skated LA w/ Donny and Bowl (filmed w/ ortiz) BIRDLAND | 3 VCI w/Kosick | 4 hung out at Birdhouse house | 5 hung out w/ GRECKO and ALI | 6 night skyle w/ Kerry | 7 PATCHES PARTY (drunk muska) | 8 Skips Ditch BIRDLAND |
|---|---|---|---|---|---|---|
| CALIFORNIA | CALIFORNIA | CALIFORNIA | CALIFORNIA | CALIFORNIA | CALIFORNIA | CALIFORNIA |
| 9 NEW MOON CRUISED AROUND HB | 10 BOULALA ARRIVED | 11 Went to brethowd SKIPS DITCH w/ Boulala, cairns, alan, Pete | 12 GIANT MINI Hung out w/ RUNE, ALI, and ALI BIRDLAND | 13 BERLYL AND SHIT (Photos w/kosick) | 14 hung out w/ Boulala | 15 Photos w/ kosick |
| CALIFORNIA | CALIFORNIA | CALIFORNIA | CALIFORNIA | CALIFORNIA | CALIFORNIA | CALIFORNIA |
| 16 mt baldy whole pipe, nikel vats CALIFORNIA | 17 CATALINA IS. CALIFORNIA St. Patrick's Day | 18 LEFT FOR SAN FRANSISCO (chris senn's) | 19 Skated SF (Adrenalin house) | 20 Yuba City skatepark Vernal Equinox | 21 SACTO w/BA | 22 The Avenues → |
| 23 Skated SF grinded double kink (Filmed w/ SATVA) Palm Sunday | 24 FULL MOON went to DELUXE, took photos w/ LUKE → | 25 JIMS RAMP JAM | 26 S.F. hills w/ Cairns, grecs,cairns Boulala, Ernando Moul | 27 Flew to LA, went to big brother (Jamie thomas) interveiw | 28 volcom (talked to remy about NIKE) wax ledges | 29 RIVERSIDE photos/w kosick |
| 30 hunting to a pau w/ Jamie wax ledges w/ moul, baulala Easter Sunday | 31 skated ledges chilled w/ muska at etnies Easter Monday | | | Good Friday | | → |

*OUTHOUSES* **CALIFORNIA**

2K  S  0 3  jimmy pager

# .IL 1997

ALI CAIRNS C 32 1 98 011 44 23 98 Wallacavage 245 59 610 96 Shrimka 4 35 4

| MONDAY | TUESDAY | WEDNESDAY | THURSDAY | FRIDAY | SATURDAY |
|---|---|---|---|---|---|
| Alex Moul jackman close abingdon oxon OX M 01 5 03 | 1 Tum yeto (got package) CALIFORNIA April Fool's Day | 2 wax legdos GIANT RAMP w/ Vallely | 3 Skated schools w/ vallely, boulala ed, moul, lowery, ortiz night skate w/ reynolds and bubla | 4 GIANT RAMP filmed w/ cheryl grogin w/ Andrew reynolds + mike | 5 Toy machine Demo go tarts w/ zero team and boogie |
| 7 HUNG OUT WITH THE BIRD HOUSE HOUSE NEW MOON | 8 fairmans cleaned my Fucking room | 9 mall w/ SEth Joe + Heid saw GIAR HAR DAY | 10 finished photo's went to Philly +snuckskate on school | 11 Battle 'o' the bands ali's has house | 12 Get Nike Package went to Ywcate SKC 4 tournan went to cliffs went to rich's stayed at rich's + henners |
| 14 Went to fairmans CAMPPACIT ARRIVED went to mikes w/ Joe went to shrimka w/ Barrel | 15 Shot Photo w/ wallacavage Laundess Hey Car drop in, duct bowl Footage w/ Joe | 16 went to worcleton yet skated vic w/ Joe Skates+stark weather hung out w/ brannart filmed | 17 went to Jayson's hung out w/ kandice | 18 Fairmans went to CFS and ate macdonalds went to ali's w/ mike Saw CHASING with mark | 19 went to Jay's hung out w/ kandice stayed over Jayson |
| 21 West End Skatepark | 22 ALLENTOWN LEHIGH UNIV. First Day of Passover FULL MOON | 23 hung out w/ kandice West End Skatepark stayed at kings | 24 West End skatepark hung out w/ bran OIL | 25 went to Philly hung w/ kandice funny Carm w/ Dercato Arbor Day | 26 North New Jersey (skated a pool) Timmytown 6 and TM STAYS |
| 28 franks w/ bran went to Ridley Hill w/ Tim + mike TM STAYED | 29 TRENTON NJ | 30 Philadelphia w/ Tim ALS HOUSE starkweather | | | |

ORDER FRICKSON 302 90 CR

MARCH

| | | | | | | 1 |
|---|---|---|---|---|---|---|
| 2 | 3 | 4 | 5 | 6 | 7 | 8 |
| 9 | 10 | 11 | 12 | 13 | 14 | 15 |
| 16 | 17 | 18 | 19 | 20 | 21 | 22 |
| 23 | 24 | 25 | 26 | 27 | 28 | 29 |
| 30 | 31 | | | | | |

MAY

| | | | | | 1 | 2 | 3 |
|---|---|---|---|---|---|---|---|
| 4 | 5 | 6 | 7 | 8 | 9 | 10 |
| 11 | 12 | 13 | 14 | 15 | 16 | 17 |
| 18 | 19 | 20 | 21 | 22 | 23 | 24 |
| 25 | 26 | 27 | 28 | 29 | 30 | 31 |

cong inc attn steve THOUSES mills/scott mceachen rman drive bequerton 97005

13

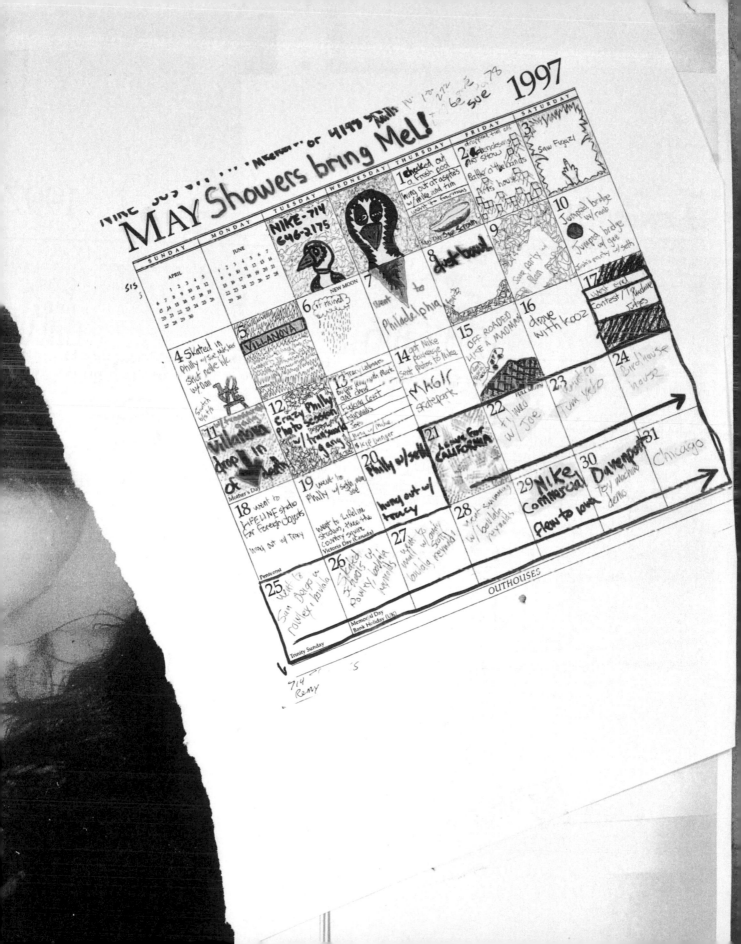

# JUNE 1997

AirHitch
1-800-3__ -2__

| SUNDAY | MONDAY | TUESDAY | WEDNESDAY | THURSDAY | FRIDAY | SATURDAY |
|---|---|---|---|---|---|---|
| 1 Bloomington INDIANA | 2 Cincinatti | 3 Cincinatti | 4 South Bend | 5 NEW MOON Lansing Michigan | 6 Brighton Michigan | 7 Pittsburgh |
| 8 West Virginia | 9 Baltimore hung out w/ Jess mark and bran | 10 hung out w Kooz and Branton met at fairmans went to New England | 11 Laconia New Hampshire | 12 Massachusetts | 13 hung w/ Bran (prank calls) went to fairm Seth, Brian Golfed w/ chris H. | 14 went to ocean City MD Flag Day |
| 15 OCEAN CITY MD. Father's Day | 16 golfed w/ Kooz/steve m Went to Philly Park new wall | 17 ran errands went to the driving range & Seth went to Jess w/ mike | 18 Twooked truck immuriature golf w/ chrith harina went and got golf balls w/ chris | 19 went to Philly Park hung w/ bran prank calls golfed + skated at stru w/h mike, seth, bran wentto Adams party golfed at penn oak | 20 FULL MOON chilled w/ Mike & Perry skated philly park went swimming at s went to Mandy party Edited Joe skated @parkine atstru | 21 Phoenixville Bridge hung w/ Kooz Jen Jones party some party w/ je swimming at stru sue and Irene St. were Summer Solstice |
| 22 Watched fotage with Joe Philly Park swimming at ryans | 23 I cant Remember | 24 jumped on trampoline went to granite run w/ bran hung out w/ ryan dbe Picked up Irene St. Jean Baptiste Fête Nationale des Québeçois | 25 ran mile w/ bran + Jess! stereo and chap at Philly Park Ryans Pool party | 26 niced out w/ gee and Mike went to ryans hung out w/ Jess and deron went Raven/chris | 27 | 28 philly Park mike tyson fight mad heads at m crib |
| 29 chilled at my house w/ gee, mike, Hussi Irene, raab, ryan, sue Blah Blah Blah | 30 Great Adventure w/ irene ryan, sue, alex taylor, nicole | | | | MAY<br>1 2 3<br>4 5 6 7 8 9 10<br>11 12 13 14 15 16 17<br>18 19 20 21 22 23 24<br>25 26 27 28 29 30 31 | JULY<br>1 2 3 4<br>6 7 8 9 10 11<br>13 14 15 16 17 18<br>20 21 22 23 24 25<br>27 28 29 30 31 |

*OUTHOUSES*

# BAM MARGERA

| SUNDAY | MONDAY | TUESDAY | WEDNESDAY | THURSDAY | FRIDAY | SATURDAY |
|---|---|---|---|---|---|---|
| | | **1** Portland oregon | **2** Portland Burnside | **3** hung out w/ raab then bran, then mike, alyssa, kerry | **4** NEW MOON 4th of July Party at Philly Park hung out at Kims **Independence Day** | **5** Skated Philly w/ kerry, alyssa, seber, Leo, gee Party at Jen Jones Marshmallows at very house w/ gee Leo and everyone |
| ...kerrylan ...e, alyssa ...d seber ...to angies ...XFORD | **7** Fairman's hung w/ bran a cool fight intown hung out w/ HEATH went to sarahs went skating at Starfsweather | **8** went to steves w/ kooz | **9** leave for europe | **10** OXFORD ENGLAND w/ Alex Moul | **11** LONDON ENGLAND London Arena competition → | **12** LONDON ENGLAND |
| ...NDON ...LLAND | **14** LONDON ENGLAND harrow skatepk and Oxford | **15** HOLLAND BELGIUM AND GERMANY | **16** PRAHA PRAGUE CZECH REP | **17** PRAGUE CZECH REP | **18** PRAGUE CZECH REP | **19** PRAGUE CZECH REP |
| FULL MOON ...RAGUE ...ECH REP ...n Place ...600 | **21** BERLIN GERMANY | **22** COPENHAGEN DENMARK | **23** COPENHAGEN DENMARK | **24** COPENHAGEN DENMARK STOCKHOLM sweeden | **25** STOCKHOLM sweeden | **26** STOCKHOLM sweeden |
| ...OCKHOLM sweeden | **28** STOCKHOLM sweeden | **29** STOCKHOLM SWEEDEN | **30** STOCKHOLM TO ↓ HOME hung w/ kooz | **31** hung w/ fix went to Jackies w/ bran Jess Gosker Fair | **JUNE** <br> 1 2 3 4 5 6 7 <br> 8 9 10 11 12 13 14 <br> 15 16 17 18 19 20 21 <br> 22 23 24 25 26 27 28 <br> 29 30 | **AUGUST** <br> 1 2 <br> 3 4 5 6 7 8 9 <br> 10 11 12 13 14 15 16 <br> 17 18 19 20 21 22 23 <br> 24 25 26 27 28 29 30 <br> 31 |

OUTHOUSES

BAM

| SUNDAY | MONDAY | TUESDAY | WEDNESDAY | THURSDAY | FRIDAY | SATURDAY |
|---|---|---|---|---|---|---|
| JULY / SEPTEMBER (mini calendars) | Fuck the Fuck off! | Every name Chris Raab ever had: 1. Kraz 2. Cantaloe 3. Kooz 4. Case 5. Rabe 6. Chris Red | 7. Fix 8. Coot 9. Con Air 10. Cossatter 11. chwissywissy | Kooz Pager 9631702 | 1 chilled w/ Con Air watched slingblade w/ Jackie Al's Cocktail Party w/ Irene | 2 hung w/ fis down, horvath MET went to Paff ryan hanna went to cl till 600am |
| 3 Lenape went swimming at steves chilled w/ Michelle ran w/ chris FIRST KISS | 4 went to BK w/ Jess, bran Faurmans chilled w/ Mike Ryan chilled w/ Middle New York | 5 watched scream~ ryan own went to Alicia's house to chill | 6 skated w/ kerry mike DEFINETLY KILL YOURSELF went to sives went to Joes | 7 TOM PAGES ↓ | 8 chris Raab is a fuckhead and Friday night is so cool TGIF | 9 hung out w/ Blind/menace guys. went to phil w/ michelle |
| 10 went to philly hung out w/ stevie Lavar and spencer went to Dawns got dialer from zak chilled w/ art | 11 Kooz needs ICE CREAM Jogged w/ Jess | 12 went to Granite run w/ Michelle chilled at sives w/ Dave Kyle | 13 Fucked w/ shit at radio shack brandon | 14 went to Bob's w/ michelle then ryan | 15 Fucking party or something | 16 swam w/ racal drove fuc to philly |
| 17 red lobster w/ Jess ryan kooz | 18 I give a Fuck? went to wildwood FULL MOON | 19 WILD Fukin Wood SAW Heath buddy and Pete | 20 Mall + EVENT HORIZON w/ MICHELLE TO DERON'S HOUSE WE WENT | 21 Errands w/ raab + Dom Got wireless mic watched movie w/ Michelle Philly Traab | 22 chilled w/ kooz ryan childers house | 23 ryan nee shoes went to shawns party Mid |
| 24 Photo Shoot with Michelle deron Mark Tra 31 chilled w/ Michelle then ryan | 25 went to Philly w/ Joe | 26 hung out w/ Michelle OFF ROADED WITH GEE AND RAAB | 27 hey dick HEADS GOT A NEW BED Kony n ARE BAKE GOLFING w/ Kooz, brian Joe OUTHOUSES | 28 skated w/ mike, kooz chilled w/ deron Jess, kooz GOT THUNDER BOX AND NIKE CATALOG | 29 went to Philly w/ Joe + Mike Dude, you're gay | 30 went to philly skated w/ TIM michelles party bowling w/ Jess/Jen Amores |

Q: Why is Everyone getting a Fucking PAGER?

# SEPTEMBER 1997

**OUTHOUSES**

| SUNDAY | MONDAY | TUESDAY | WEDNESDAY | THURSDAY | FRIDAY | SATURDAY |
|---|---|---|---|---|---|---|
| Chrissy Farin (NIKE) 1 503 3 | **1** NEW MOON Went to Tinicum Sk8prk then to Matt's in Mary land then watched phila ports w/ bran Labor Day | **2** Philly Park w/ Malgatoydo haircut and McD's w/ michelle | **3** tied up a bee w/ kooz, bran, mike and Joe hung out w/ bran shawn, karr at dir Gee brought photos | **4** went to Valley Fucking Forge to find out that there isnt shit to film there. QUNN CAME OVER TO CHILL | **5** went to Philly Park hung out w/ Michelle went to some Party | **6** Went to Jens w/ Joe TALKED ON THE PHONE fuck Jess + HANNA's freds FIRE |
| **7** chilled w/ Michelle RAGED PHILLY PARK! went to Ellas w/ michelle went to ARTS + TEA | **8** went to EAST Owen Cairmans Wallacavage Come over went to Valley Forge w/ kerry, Jake Joe + others | **9** trapped Kerry in the bathroom, Cairmans w/ kerry + mike chilled w/ ryan dunn went to Williams w/ shrinkm Long walk w/ chris H went to eat w/ bran + Jess | **10** to EAST TO TOWN TO HANNA'S TO HOME TO BED TO SLEEP. | **11** Picked up Michelle from school chilled w/ ryan dunn went to Emersons Party | **12** Filmed in Philly w/ Joe, mike Boich, bach Member Philly Park cruise night and saw Money Talks w/ Michelle | **13** Judged a Contest at westend chrissy wiggy came over Langs Party w/ michelle |
| **14** Raab sent himself over went to Fein thyme and Joes w/ Michelle SAW UTOPIE 1997 | **15** PHILLY PARK FILM SESSION! SAW "THE GAME" w/ MICHELLE to JOES, to HANNA's, to BED | **16** FULL MOON Fucking Dentist! Community Service The Mall to trade shoes w/ Michelle to Michelle's went to Jaysons TOP 10 LIST FOR ED | **17** FILMED AT PHILLY PARK PICKED UP MICHELLE FROM WORK w/ SETH TALKED TO MICHELLE FOR SEVERAL HRS. ABOUT GOOD STUFF! ♥ RAAB SAID " I LOVE YOU" | **18** Philly park cast FUCKED MICHELLE ★ "I LOVE YOU" | **19** something w/ michelle raab doesnt look tuff scwl anymore football game and Joes | **20** Community Service saw Wishmaster w/ michelle, devon, Jess mike, family Party w/ Sue, chilled w/ ryan dunn |
| **21** restaurant festival w/ michelle and Philly Parke chilled w/ Con Air K-mart w/ michelle and sisters saw CLUTCH | **22** went to East Skated Philly w/ mike, joe, kerry hit a 007 BMW w/ skateboard Logged footy at Joes w/ kerry mike and bauchan Autumnal Equinox | **23** chilled w/ Kerry picked up Mich-elle from school and fucked today ★ | **24** worked on video at Joes w/ mike + kerry hung out w/ Michelle this symbol means I fucked went to Jays | **25** ATLANTIC CITY trade show w/ TIM, GEE, ADAM emersons party snuck out michelle ★ grandparents heard some uh giggling | **26** Philly Park (540) hung w/ Michelle went to Joes w/ Mike, Bamrod an early nap. | **27** Community Service Philly Park (Blunt on wall) (bucky, Agah, dove gee, kuroe) picked up Michelle |
| **28** 5th market Philly Drop In A party at my house ★ | **29** BAMMO MICHELLE DAY PRANK CALLS w/ BRANDON | **30** school to community to pick up Michelle to home to East side mom's to Michelle to home Bran came over | Note to Self ~ My girlfriend is better than yours! | | AUGUST  1 2  3 4 5 6 7 8 9  10 11 12 13 14 15 16  17 18 19 20 21 22 23  24 25 26 27 28 29 30  31 | OCTOBER  1 2 3 4  5 6 7 8 9 10 11  12 13 14 15 16 17 18  19 20 21 22 23 24 25  26 27 28 29 30 31 |

19

# OCTOBER

★'s FUCKED MICHELLE

·3  9 Geoff
9  75 G.

skated w/ Mike

TOM BOYLE
215 · 7 5 2t
PAGE 800

|  | | | | | |
|---|---|---|---|---|---|
| **SUNDAY** | **MONDAY** | **TUESDAY** | **WEDNESDAY** | **THURSDAY** | **FRIDAY** |

|  | | | | | |
|---|---|---|---|---|---|
| **SEPTEMBER**<br>1 2 3 4 5 6<br>7 8 9 10 11 12 13<br>14 15 16 17 18 19 20<br>21 22 23 24 25 26 27<br>28 29 30 | **NOVEMBER**<br>1<br>2 3 4 5 6 7 8<br>9 10 11 12 13 14 15<br>16 17 18 19 20 21 22<br>23 24 25 26 27 28 29<br>30 | VOLCOM 714<br>Remy S  '55<br>Mark CAFFEY<br>4 0<br>Pro___on Pl.<br>Newport beach, CA<br>9  63 | **1** NEW MOON | **2** w/ Michelle<br>Picked her up, to<br>Nussex, to dinner<br>at her house to<br>LIAR LIAR! to sta-<br>dium grille to<br>childers to ★.<br>WENT TO PHILLY<br>Rosh Hashana (5758) | **3** TO VOCEATI<br>NE PHILL<br>HAUNTED HAYA<br>w/ MICHELLE<br>22 OTHER PEO |
| **5** Hang out w/Michelle ★<br>TENNESSEE<br>(NASHVILLE) | **6** MEMPHIS<br>TENNESSEE<br>Graceland<br>to Nashville | **7** CHATTANOOGA<br>TENNESSEE ○ | **8** CHATTANOOGA<br>TENNESSEE ○ | **9** GATLINBURG<br>TENNESSEE ○ | **10** WENT D EAS<br>TO BRANDON<br>UPS w/ JESS (Newfoun<br>Set up drums<br>side w/ JESSE<br>HANN<br>Cheese C__<br>w/ Michelle<br>chilled w/ Ro |
| **12** Philly Park<br>w/ Kerry +<br>★ Michelle<br>chilled w/ Chaab<br>and Michelle<br>to Joes | **13** chilled over Mike<br>at Philly Park<br>Doofs Party w/<br>Michelle<br>Columbus Day<br>(Observed)<br>Thanksgiving Day<br>(Canada) to Joes | **14** Philly Park<br>+ West Philly<br>to Michelles<br>to Joes | **15** West END<br>Skatepark<br>snuck Michelle<br>out ★ | **16** FULL MOON<br>went EAST<br>went to Jaysons<br>w/ Michelle<br>★ | **17** went to<br>City an<br>Philly Par<br>WENT TO EA<br>Homecoming<br>game w/<br>Mich |
| **19** ★ ★ ★<br>And The Nail<br>fourmans (New<br>Board)<br>to Starkweather w/<br>Seth and Brian<br>to Hams | **20** Skated City<br>Hall and Philly<br>Park w/ Gee, Joe, Seth<br>Menser and Kalis | **21** TO EAST, CHILLED<br>w/ BRAVO<br>KING O'FUCK IN RU-<br>SSIA<br>MALL NOTE TO SELF:<br>ALYSSA ARRIVES<br>WITH AT 8:00<br>CHRIS H. | **22** Scott T. Hut<br>dimitry, NY<br>Took Michelle to<br>Work.<br>Made Video<br>at Joes | **23** Philly<br>Park<br>Ed arriv__<br>over michelles<br>for lo bm<br>To Emerson<br>Party | **24** Phil<br>Park<br>E<br>★ ★<br>I KNOW<br>WHAT YO<br>DID LAST SU__<br>w/ Michelle |
| **26** To Philly w/<br>Michelle<br>FASHION SHOOT<br>w/ ED, DEANNA<br>MICHELLE, QUIM<br>GEE WILLIAM BRI<br>IN PHILLY ★<br>Daylight Savings Time<br>Ends (2:00 AM)<br>HUNG W/ KOOZ | **27** Philly<br>Park and<br>Night City<br>Session | **28** To Lehigh<br>w/ Kerry, Mike,<br>Ed, deanna,<br>Gee, Wall__<br>and ELYSSA<br>Nollie lip by me | **29** 9:00 am<br>we sneak<br>MD's meeting<br>w/ Brian + Mal<br>to East<br>Philly<br>Jamie and Adrian<br>Arrives | **30** Philly Park<br>and City<br>watched footage at<br>Joes<br>★ ★<br>stayed at Michelles | **31** NEW M__<br>6:00 am<br>Skate mission<br>Philly w/ Jamie<br>mike<br>Eli__<br>road<br>ky<br>cam<br>stayed at Mi__<br>Halloween baby birt |

*OUTHOUSES*

AMC ___ AMC PAIN
556  5 5  ·4

SATURDAY

ENT ON A
MISSION
W/ RAAB

worthtown
MN
MICHELLE
TO CHILDERS

lly Park

KISS THE GIRLS
michelle, Raab
d kwn chris did
their movie is called
Raab a moore
ran errands
in a computer
es ollie
Gee, John an

MECOMING!
★

FINALLY!

5
illed w/ED +
anna and
002
★
Horeen Party
Michelle, Christ

21

# DECEMBER 1997

OUTHOUSES

| SUNDAY | MONDAY | TUESDAY | WEDNESDAY | THURSDAY | FRIDAY | SATURDAY |
|---|---|---|---|---|---|---|
| | **1** VISITED MICHELLE AT EAST. TO EXTON MALL W/BRAND. PICKED UP RAAB FROM CFS. WENT TO MICHELLE'S TILL 10:00. WATCHED A MOVIE W/ROUNDHOUND + RAABS. FILMED W/BRAND, ART, JESS + CHRIS H. | **2** TO EAST. PHILLY PARK. SHOPPING W/MICHELLE AT EXTON. WENT OVER RAABS | **3** TO EAST-TO FAIRMANS. PHILLY PARK. BROKE BOTH TRUCKS. TO GEES TO WATCH A VIDEO THAT WAS EVEN FUCKING RECORDED. | **4** TO EAST FAIRMANS SHOPPING SPREE. HANG OUT W/MICHELLE ★★ WENT TO PHILLY (A PORTRAIT W/ GEE) AND KALIS. | **5** Philly Park. took Michelle to work. chilled w/chris R. till 3:00 am. chilled w/ jess chm + devon till 5:00 | **6** Went to Philly Park. Internet w/ teali sandi and gee. MIKE VALLELY'S SPOKEN WORDS At SUBZERO. went over Michelle's chris + kim came over |
| **7** ★★ went to Philly w/ Michelle. Skated Philly Park. Went to gee's w/ Tim, dun + kenny. went to South Street. The drive ★ home was fun. chilled course I ground my foot at FDR | **8** Took Michelle to work. Fairmans. Picked up chris from school - went to his house as Jill cooked a meal. dan, kenny, and mike came over. watched austin powers | **9** TO EAST. RAINBOW W/ DERON ANETHEMA. FAXED SHIT AT FAIRMANS. went to Ashas w/ Michelle. went to chris's | **10** hung out w/ michelle ★★ Went over Jens and lukes | **11** Left for HAWAII. skated kona half pipe | **12** Volcom demo (at Waikiki) alan peterson + kale Black Flys Party | **13** North Shore (sunset beach) |
| **14** FULL MOON. North shore (Surf contest) | **15** North shore. cruised around honolulu w/ dustin + traian bank. stayed at klints | **16** chilled in Honolulu. skated a pool w/ Neil, kale, min and Remy and friends | **17** took a boat to an island w/ Dustin klint, Jen and Patty | **18** Flew to Maui w/ Remy, Clint, dustin Jen, kale | **19** Volcom demo at (mall skateditch). mini ramp demo (skated). drove to a large mountain w/ crater | **20** Volcom demo at Maui Park |
| **21** came home from hawaii. Went to mall w/ Michelle (chris + kim came over) hung out w/ Michelle + thed w/ Raab. Winter Solstice | **22** TODAY KICKED ASS. watched a movie w/ michelle. raab came over. took Michelle out for 1 hour | **23** went to town for shopping w/ Jessard Michelle. dan w/ and Aspile came over and w/ to (michelle). saw TITANIC w/ michelle, Dan, Aspile, raab + Kim. went to Jim w/ jess | **24** went to rainbow ran into christtsaakem. listened to oil mix chilled w/ Jess + Devon. Dinner at Michelles. went to my house (x-mas eve party) gee comin over. went to Alis party w/ Michelle and gee in sportscar. First Day of Hanukkah | **25** opened things. went to Michelles. had to leave early. Sue down ★★ Christmas | **26** The worst day of my life, then after 5:00 it started too get better. to mall w/ Michelle. Saw american Wolf in Paris. picked shit at Boxing Day Mall | **27** Fairmans living out w/ Aspile + went to Joes. went for Nells neighbor w/ chris kim scott devon Wil and scott |
| **28** Went to the BEACH and mall w/ Michelle, Jess, Lisa and mom on the way home ★★. went to house where mom was housesitting it was a party | **29** NEW MOON. TO The Bram house w/ michelle. went to granite run and ran into her mom and sisters ★. listened to Oil record in basement, worked on calendar | **30** Went to kinkos w/ Michelle for calendar Fairmans, Macdonalds. watched Sleeping w/ enemy w/ michelle ★. watched chasing amy w/hanna, Raab, kim devon, Jess chilled w/ Raab till 3:00 | **31** went to family's w/ Jess and Michelle. went to Philly w/ Macbride + Jess. took photos w/ wallace Rob erichelson. chilled w/ Devon, Jess went to michelles for New Years. Jan miss at new party. went to Boots ★ | | | |

With the unedjucating combination of me skipping school every other day to go skateboarding with Mike Maldonado and getting suspended for drawing picture of Mr. Nutting eating out Mark Hannas ass I probably made it ~~to class on an average of 2 to 3 days a week. I was so~~

and getting suspended for drawing pictures of ~~the~~ class eating out Mark Hannas ass I probably made to ~~school~~ an average of 2 to 3 days a week, I was so behind with homework and tests I felt it wasnt even worth going anymore!

BAM @ B³ GREGOR

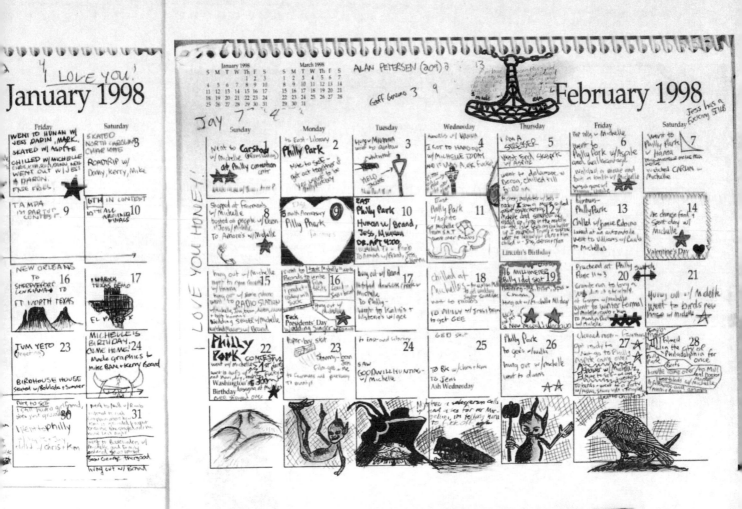

January 1998

"I LOVE YOU!"

February 1998

Page 29

# March 1998

More Skates: 717- -0-E 3  Christie fax (503) 6 1 6
BIRD- 9 0 7   SEBER: 717-6-4- 1
(714) 5 0 7 VOLCOM FAX

Tim (guy from Tv show)
(714) 3 5 5  Ro Gilmer in Pa

LANCASTER SKATE PARK - 717- 3 45  STEVE MOORE: 6 -89

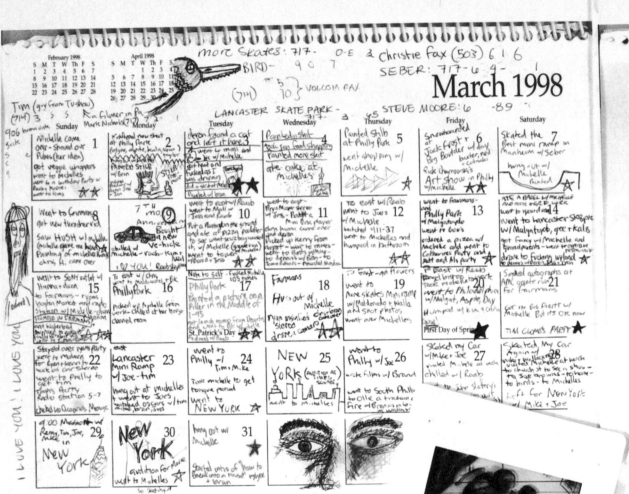

84

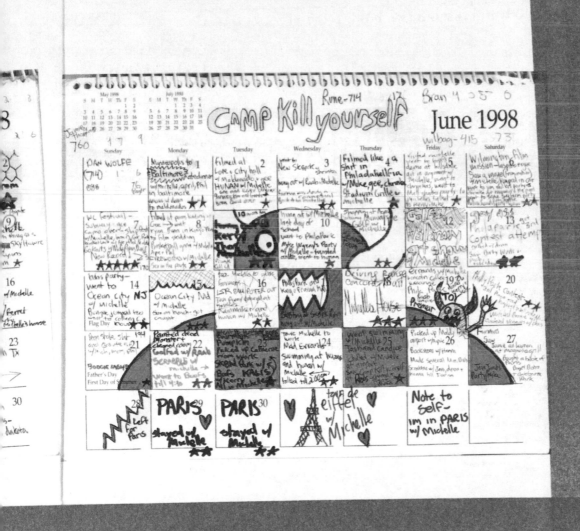

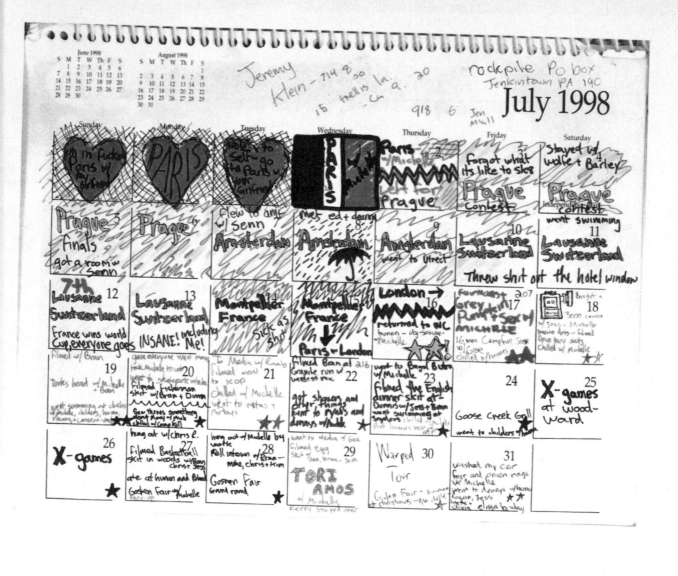

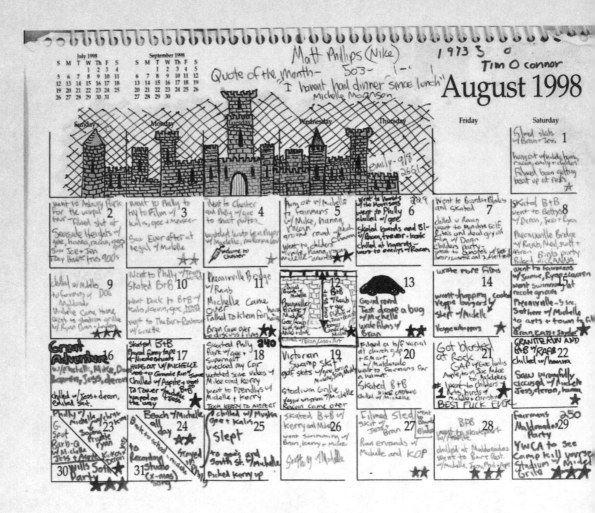

September 1998

Page 37

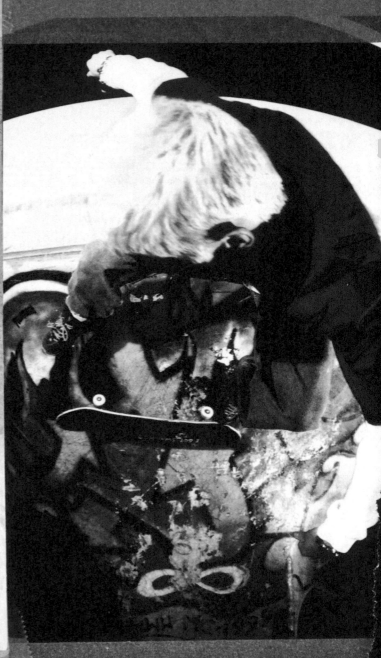

BK virginia fall

Punches, slaps + falls

*Switch*

1. Maldonado down the stairs
2. Maldonado hit w/ pillow
3. Jess getting slaped
4. Bran punching me about people
5. Bam punching bran
6. Bam punching bran + gee
7. slap + slap
8. punch
9. you got a bowling ball
10. dropping tv
11. Punching window
12. on the roof
13. I cant open it
14. Texaco slap
15. Texaco punch
16. Dun getting beat up
17. Bran + dunn fighting at New years

24. fan fall
25. Fan fall 2
26. golf fall
27. Media
28. punching bran at oakbo
29. english skit punches
30. jump into bush
31. umbrella jump
32. Bran Getting beat up

Robahouse

33. syracuse bed smack
34. Toys R us bran
35. Toys #2
36. Brans lamp fall
37. Bran lawyer shit

# October 1998

September 1998

| S | M | T | W | Th | F | S |
|---|---|---|---|---|---|---|
|   |   | 1 | 2 | 3 | 4 | 5 |
| 6 | 7 | 8 | 9 | 10 | 11 | 12 |
| 13 | 14 | 15 | 16 | 17 | 18 | 19 |
| 20 | 21 | 22 | 23 | 24 | 25 | 26 |
| 27 | 28 | 29 | 30 |   |   |   |

November 1998

| S | M | T | W | Th | F | S |
|---|---|---|---|---|---|---|
| 1 | 2 | 3 | 4 | 5 | 6 | 7 |
| 8 | 9 | 10 | 11 | 12 | 13 | 14 |
| 15 | 16 | 17 | 18 | 19 | 20 | 21 |
| 22 | 23 | 24 | 25 | 26 | 27 | 28 |
| 29 | 30 |   |   |   |   |   |

| Sunday | Monday | Tuesday | Wednesday | Thursday | Friday | Saturday |
|---|---|---|---|---|---|---|
|  |  |  |  | **1** | **2** Corn Maze w/ Maldo, Aspite, Jess, Racan / BFB / chilled w/ Michelle | **3** Installed Car w/ Ryan O. kung fu fest / BFB w/ Maldonado / Hunan w/ Mike + Jess Mark hannas ★ |
| **4** Pep boys, Rainbow Circuitcity and Michelles → (Contest) ★ | **5** Lunch w/ hanna & Racan / To Michelles Mall w/ devon → Scanning CDs / Teaques / Gee stayed over | **6** Kung fu skit at Quarry / Bron to Michelles / Gee stayed over | **7** Filmed in cornfield w/ Gee / Went to Philly / Kara and Mans Lost w/ Michelle in her car → ★ | **8** tied devon to a pole w/ gee at BFB / fairmans w/ Mike drove Michelle home / BFB session to Arts w/ Bron | **9** Bistro w/ hanna Racan / Jess's drums in the highway / chilled w/ Michelle + gee + racan + bron / Arrival from Killers Filmed hall scene in basement ★ | **10** Malls w/ Raab / nunan w/ Mich, Raab + Kim / HOMECOMING To Melissa's, home then Mikey — ★ |
| **11** Dilworthtown stuff Quarry Jump w/ Michelle white dave goes to hanna / Naked dave Photos w/ michelle ★ | **12** errands → / to Michelles Columbus Day / BFB and Josh's Thanksgiving Day (Canada) 5-6 party bron come over | **13** Fairmans 5:30 / 16mm w/ Michelle Hanna & Layne / Bretts Jump w/ gee mike, Sue mandy Dina + edital ★★ | **14** Fairmans 3:87 to show w/ Michelle to Mall / More Skates w/ Kerry + Lindsay ★ | **15** BFB Josh + Aspite | **16** Granite Run / Anastasia on ice w/ Mich, christina + bron / Boss's Day ★ | **17** Philly w/ Maldonado / china ledges / chilled w/ Michelle ★ |
| **18** to day days hung out w/ Michelle to hannas to IRON HILL / BFB ★ | **19** Court Skated Philly w/ Aspite / BFB | **20** To Fed Ex BFB + Skit / haunted hayride w/ Michelle + Racan chilled | **21** Filmed w/ Joe + aspite in Philly to Michelles / BFB sword skit / Ed + deanna chilled | **22** kmart w/ ed + deanna Mikes house / filmed at BFB w/ ed / Mikes Party mikes b.day ★ | **23** BFB + Mall / hayride w/ Ade + Melissa ★★ | **24** BFB / fairmans chilled w/ Melissa + Kev / West end w/ Mike + Kerry |
| **25** Raked leaves Mall w/ hanna chilly / Pep boys + subway git / Raab — mark hannas git + granite run Daylight Saving w/ Mich Time Ends Kerry ★ | **26** Hung out w/ Raab all Jay granite run mall w/ michelle / Hag vite w/ michelle & cousins | **27** Philly w/ Mike + Kerry) and now w/ michelle / Mall w/ Jethltull / Philly again Skated w/ Kerry ★ | **28** BFB w/ ed, deanna, mike Kerry + spazbite to Michelles / Shopping cart Madbran, ed Jess Noss aspite ★ | **29** Birdhouse video took Michelle to Work / west end skaßk w/ ed, deanna, mike, kerry Müllerlane + hoof bite | **30** BFB w/ mike + dacutts / big fight w/ mich | **31** BFB / Birds party w/ Michi Jess ed + deanna / Halloween ★★ |

| | October 1998 | December 1998 |
|---|---|---|
| | S M T W Th F S | S M T W Th F S |
| | 1 2 3 | 1 2 3 4 5 |
| | 4 5 6 7 8 9 10 | 6 7 8 9 10 11 12 |
| | 11 12 13 14 15 16 17 | 13 14 15 16 17 18 19 |
| | 18 19 20 21 22 23 24 | 20 21 22 23 24 25 26 |
| | 25 26 27 28 29 30 31 | 27 28 29 30 31 |

TY evans

619

| Sunday | Monday | Tuesday | Wednesday | Thursday | Friday | Saturday |
|---|---|---|---|---|---|---|
| **1** chilled w/ Raab Pizza w/ Mike, raab, hanna, racan chilled at home ★★ | **2** Filmed 16mm of shopping carts w/ bran, gee, Joss chilled w/ michelle and went to day days To arts for voices | **3** Granite run w/ michelle developed film went to bfb w/ Mike Election Day ★ | **4** Granite run helped ed w/ Art shit Skated w/ Kalis, steve Gee at temple rainbow records | **5** Concord mall Locked keys in car broke window w/a fucking brick Ged shit at Michelles chilled w/ Deron | **6** Skits + 16mm w/ bran + gee Eds Art show w/ Michelle + Mayer | **7** chilled w/ michelle Washington D.C. ★ |
| **8** Memphis, TN | **9** Little Rock, AK | **10** Arizona | **11** CALIFORNIA Veterans Day chilled at elisa's Remembrance Day (Canada) Boobala | **12** Skated HB w/ Reynolds, Kerry Sumner | **13** Ventura Contest Jumped off roof | **14** Ventura Contest Toy flip dinner in hollywood |
| **15** La school w/ Geoff, larry, ed Kosick, arto, deann, mikes Finished stills graphic | **16** Skated w/ Geoff, arto, ed, larry, mike + elissa watched Waterboy Hollywood | **17** to dave sheridans w/ ericdeson discussed more shit — went to dinner sandiego | **18** drilled w/ Jamie Skated w/ Ty, Munford, Jamie | **19** Turn Yeto got boards Filmed w/ Jamie + Ty Smashed Face in? | **20** Get the fuck home Went to Arts | **21** Fairmans hung out w/ Ryan Dunn Saw Michelle! Arts hause ★★ |
| **22** bagel bistro w/ deron + sean chilled w/ Michelle Ryan Oldes Arts ★★ | **23** Saw enemy of the state | **24** Philly flicks w/ gee to shoot photos + 16mm chinese food w/ Michelle chilled w/ deron deep impact ★ | **25** B+B did ged stuff at Michelles Stadium Grille w/ Michelle | **26** Michelle grandmother to eat went to books w/ Michelle Thanksgiving ★★ | **27** Granite run mall w/ Michelle, bollinger, coffman B+B Exton Mall w/ michelle + dan shee Prank Calls w/ Bam, Joss, deron, Jimmy Swan + hagel | **28** 3/0 SAW JOE BLACK w/ Michelle ★ |
| **29** Rock convention w/ Michelle, Joss, mark Delaware outlets w/ Michelle + Joss ★★ | **30** Punched brag in the face at K.O.P. Saw Allyson Jaimo to Michelle's then Arts Joe's b-day | To michelles Ged test Tori amos + CKY CD mix basketball | | | | |

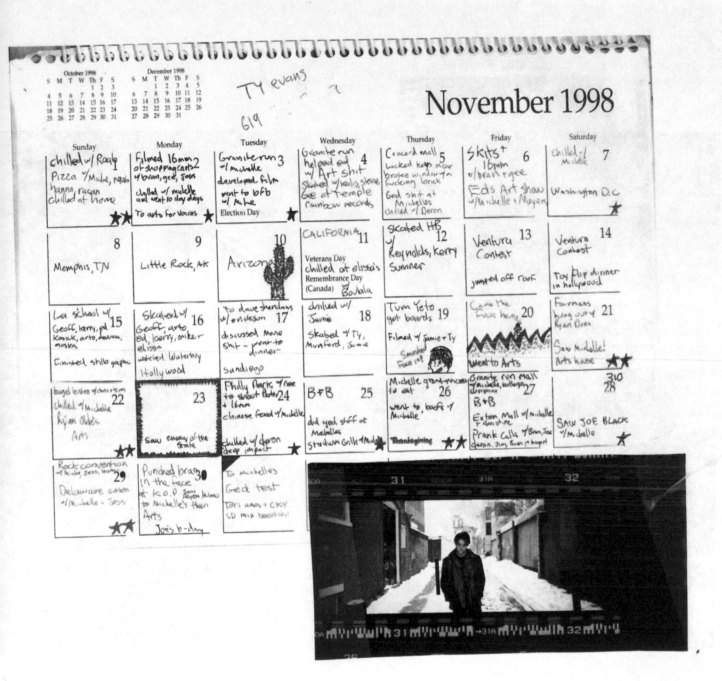

# December 1998

BAM ~ 1998-99'
© RYAN GEE PHOTO

# PHILADELPHIA

TRACADERO C

**1999'**

**HOCKEY TEMPER**
**GETZ**

DONUT QUEEN

M, Inc. • Dallas, Texas 75238-1337 ━━━ 40cm x 50cm ━━━

| | | |
|---|---|---|
| breakfast w/ missy, seth, Fauna   **3** | **4** | **5** |
| FDR<br>practice<br>for gravity<br>Games | FDR<br><br>Leave<br>for Finland<br><br>Independence Day (US) | FINLAND<br><br>Punched jean in the Face |
| **10** | **11** | **12** |
| Gravity<br>Games<br>@<br>Fdr<br>NO DRINKING! | Gravity<br>Games<br><br>film VLB pickups | Gravity<br>Games<br><br>Pissed on Tom Boyl<br><br>Party @ house |
| **17** | drove home from   **18** | EDIT<br>HIM   **19** |
| Ocean city<br>MD<br><br>Autographs | Ocean City<br>MD<br><br>WWF in Philly<br>w/ Hulk hogan | Ride bike to delawa<br><br>Gables w/ missy + Jack<br>went to Jacks House |

5

vacked out the courthouse window
cause she was pissing me off!

The benefit of drinking is
the stories you get from
the aftermath. Sober
stories and sober songs
fucking suck. the last
time I drank Jameson I broke
the fucking courthouse window
with my bare hand because
a selfish bitch and
I was fed up. I'm selfish too.
It hurt real bad then.
I went to the hospital.
but it's heald now and I'm
Laughing!

IS THE CULPRIT?

51

| 6 | 7 | 8 |
|---|---|---|
| **Drinking Binge** Crawdaddys Maximillions McKenzies | **RADIO BAM** HOOTERS w/ SHIEK | Rode quads Borders (soccer) chads ford tavern Giant more quad riding Sent tapes to MTV Al's Diamond cabaret w/ Glomb, billy, nova International Women's Day |
| 13 | 14 | 15 |
| **BARCE** SKATE! | SKATE! | SKATE! |
| **RADIO BAM** 20 **West Chester for One Day!** Antonios w/ VLTD Hooters Firewaters | Flew to La 21 **RIGHT GUARD** Commercial w/ T-OWENS METAL SHOP w/ ville, gas, Linda, Alina | 22 **RIGHT GUARD** Commercial w/ T-OWENS Dinner w/ T Hardy, ville, glom |
| | Palm Sunday Vernal Equinox 7:33 A.M. E.S.T. | |
| Drank all Day w/ ville + 27 Jonna In LA Red Rock, Barneys beanery Booze in Hotel room | Seth Builds Mansion replica 28 **HIM** MANSION IN LA RADIO BAM w/ FRANTZ IN BURBANK, CA | EDITED VLB ALL MORNIN 29 **LA** Back to HIM ma TOI restaurant |
| Easter | Easter Monday (CAN) | |

# ELEMENT TRIP 2000

Around April 2000 I met Joe Frantz at a Silly Bikini Bandits Film shoot. I remembered Adam Wallacavage telling me about a guy named Joe Frantz owned a 35mm movie camera and I was so impressed with that. I couldn't believe a random buddy owned an official movie camera. So I went up to Frantz during a lunch break and introduced myself. I told him I had $5000 in my bank account and I wanted to spend every penny on a music video for CKY. He was into it and 2 later he came to West Chester and we filmed my very first music video "96 quite bitter beings

# AUSTRALIA
## SYDNEY
## MELBOURNE
## BRISBANE

3. HOWL
4. FOOTBALL
5. SAVIOR 4:36
6. BEAT EM UP 4:25
7. TALKINGSNAKE 4:28
8. THE JERK 3:43
9. DEATH IS CERTAIN 4:2
10. GO FOR THE THRO
11. WEASELS
12. DRINK

lacrimas profundes
FILTHY NOTES FOR FROZEN

Ryan Dunn and I fly to Zurich with Glomb and
[ro]ger and we are here because I am going to
[r]ent a Ferrari for 4 days for $3,000 a day, o[ur]
mission is to get to Romania in 4 days for Red
wine out of Draculas castle in a small town cal[led]
Brasov. Driving the Ferrari through the swiss alp[s]
with one of your best friends was absolutely w[orth]
every penny of the $12,000 that MTU was stressing a[bout]
doing. It rained half of the time which pissed me
off greatly. it was such a boner killer like we
go to europe to rent a convertible ferrari
modena and if rains the whole fucking ti[me]
So Dunn and I made the best of it and put
the fucking top down in the pouring rain an[d]
decided to fly a kite like Benjamin frank[lin]
The fact we put the topdown in a rainstorm ma[de]
it way more entertaining than a beautiful
sunny day. It was the farthest yet most scen[ic]
drive i have ever been on, we had only 2 cd's [to]
listen to the entire drive which Dunn and I will h[ave]
every lyric memorized till we are Ded. Dead!
The bands were "the Beatsteaks" and the new cradle
of filth, Nyphetamine.

Once we got to Romainia I was a litt[le]
dissapointed just because it was a run[down]
3rd world shit hole with powerplants a[nd]
rabid dogs everywhere, im sure half of [them]
have never seen a paved road. frantz was
reading some facts about Romainia and he s[aid]
the average wage of romaunians per month is $70
that is absurd! Bucharest pretty much sucked a[nd]
withe everyother town except Brasov! Brasov [is]
the tourist town that they dumped all there
cash into, its such a cool looking gothic village, it
made it all worth it. Once we got to Dracula's cas[tle]
we went on a hiking mission to the top to
get some Red wine, special red wine for the
Dinner in venice. Dunn sneaks in as I wait
at the top of the Hill, he comes back 5 minu[tes]
later with 2 bottles of red wine, we are all exite[d]
and ready to celebrate for our accompléshed missio[n]
I ask dunn "was it a pain in the ass getting the wine?["]
he said "No, I got it at the gift shoppe for $6.99!"
we hopped in the bullshit ass shit ferrari and [took]
off to Venice!

BR

SOV, ROMANIA

Have A Bam! Day.
**Bam Margera**

ART WRAPPERS
@ MACH SPEED

I am at London Heathrow airport with Ryan Dunn and we both just realized that w have an 8 hour layover, 8!!!!!!!! WHO THE FUCK HAS AN 8 HOUR LAYOVER? I say to Ryan what the fuck are we going to do? he says "lets get so Annihilated drunk that we wont even remember the MTV producers that will be meeting us in 5 hours!" for some reaso his plan seemed brilliant and we went with it! A few hours go by and the crew shows up as we dont remember anything, they said 2 police officers with A.K. 47's were walking us to the airplane to make sure we didnt do anything stupid because they recognized us from "Jackass" and we were fucking hammered, just before we got on the flight I poured sugar all over Dunn then he pisse pants!

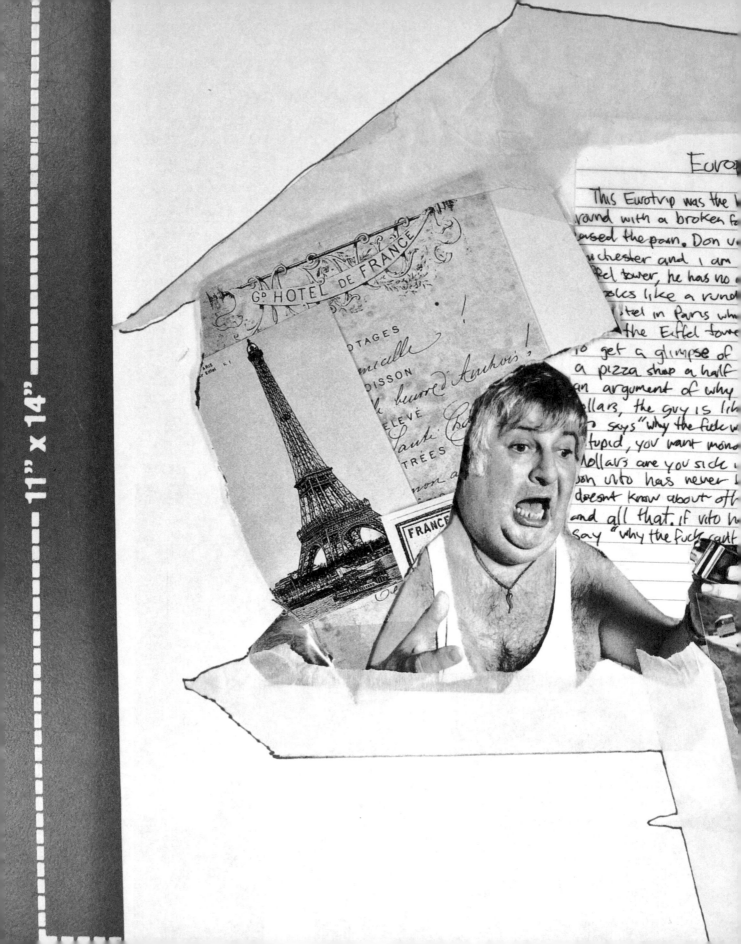

...004

he fact that I was wa...
...cked but taking don vito
...s barely been out of
...g him postcards of the
...ation towards it, he tho...
...exas oil well! we get...
...iterally 2 blocks away
...n vito didnt even go
...e farthest he walked w...
...c away and got into
...uy wouldnt take amer...
...e only take EURO!" don...
...you take money this is
...lay money but not real
... head? keep in min...
...out of the country, h...
...rrencys and languag...
...make a T-shirt i...
... one just spea...

DAVOS, SWITZERLAND
10·05

Venice was qu
because the entire
means if you have
ready to spend $50—
taxi unless you wa
filled water! One n
plenty Johnny walker
most Johnny walker
nk I have eve
tos of where I

monaco is for stu
own poodles and
is a police officer
left the dinner tab
lay down in my
over, slam my
cuff me! They
have in monaco,
no reason,
of the Mt
ail came
me, I wa
as a g
back

but very expensive.
is underwater. wh
to go anywhere g
dollars an a water
swim in the shit
decided to drink
making it the 2
check out
that night —

rich fucks whe
a Versace shit.
very block and I
to go outside and
outfit. Then 2 cops com
against the wall and hand
" what business does a six
were roughing me up for or
shouted loud enough for r
members to hear and they
rescued me. If they didnt he
bably be in a monaco prison
th no passport trying to get
merica!

FOR

Will smith party
at armory in philly
Canada Day (CAN)

6
Hellzinki,
FINLAND
film Viva la bam
w/Raab
New Moon ●

7
TALLIN
ESTONIÁ
w/Jussi from 69 eyes
we decided to do cdec on
the ferry, but it was accidentally
speed, and we were up for
2 1/2 days!
went to villas house
+ drank karhu

8
RUISROCK w/
Turbonegro + HIM

flew
to
Philly

c reeds seafood 13
Jimmy Pops
Saw Mr. and Mrs.
Smith w/missy

14

15
Edited HIM
Documentary
Turks head inn

Ocean,
MD

16" x 20"

S.A.

The reason why this photo is yellow &
gee's cat pissed all over it! Artsy!

Kick flip in Miami. I s...
Probably more faggoty then A...
Missy says J-Zac

cause

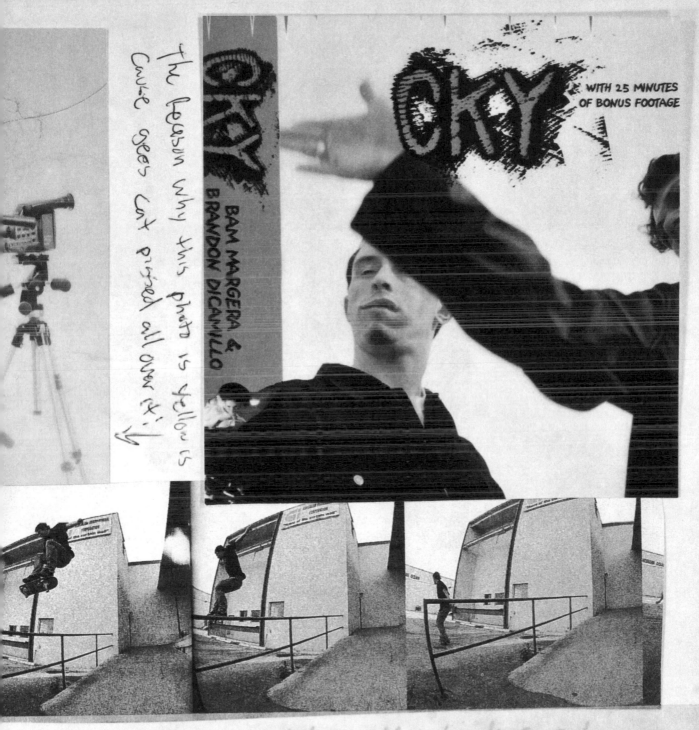

The reason why this photo is yellow is
cause Cat pissed all over it :)

OKY

OKY WITH 25 MINUTES
OF BONUS FOOTAGE

BAM MARGERA &
BRANDON DICAMILLO

Jay-2 that night, i think hes a homo
combs. Hes officially the gayest!

was Nice!

dfsskljd;slkjaeortio;lksj;dflsuperoti;

;sdfljjk sdkl;arwix;xfs dsfklixlco;o

My neighbors hated me the day I moved into my new house. It probably has a lot to do with the fact that slayer played that night. Also i forgot to show up to the welcome to the neighborhood party

Oops!

75

most of the ideas I come
up with are more complicated
to write down, so I will
just draw shitty pictures
and that is considered
my writers credit.
You can thank the red
wine on the airplanes
for that!

CKY2K

CKY
TRILOGY

CKY 3

CKY

documentary
featuring HOW TO ROB A HOUSE

Novak was willing to do whatever it took to be best man for the wedding, but technically Jess, my brother would have to be. But if Novak is willing to do anything then I should put it to the test. So I dared him to shave the top of his head off so he looks like a bald 70 year old. He did it without question. That night we went to Kildares pub and he had a hat on so it was unnoticeable. He hit on some college chicks and brought one back home and drank more beer. By the time she made it to his room his hat came off and he forgot about his terrible hairdo that causes low self esteem. He was eating her out and she looked up at him and screamed in desgust and put her clothes back on. He came out of his room unsatified and humilated and drowned his sorrows in booze!

ORIGINS: PIV

a radio show talking about how
the top of his head like an old man
a best-man in the wedding. That
to the bar with a hat on and
th his hairdo. He met a college
her back to the house. As he
out his hat came off and
table and disgusted. Novak was
had low self esteem!

OT TO FAKIE°

, your best friend? Tough
sh. i Guess that world all depend
on @the date and time like a
fuckin Rolex. @sometimes its Novak,
sometimes i want to kick his fucking face in,
I like dunn though medicine has made him
different. dice has always been the same
addicted to k-mart Ville when were around.
shit, maybe PHILLY if you'd think about
it. @ EUROPE 2004

2. fuck these motherfuckers who are
43% By Volume   who open up clothing lines
and sell the shit out with a SOOFT
billboard on sunset strip. and claim
the time, lets face it. they HAD help
THEY HAD THEM. i Scarlett !!!
Johanson... who gives a FUCK

3. store borders luck themselves down
motherfucking do stairs for Nothing!
Nothing!! fuckin Hell. Meanwhile Jude
Law is getting 2-million dollars tou memorize
27 lines in a shitty film. what happened to
the world. tiger woods hits golf balls for
millions and some motherfucker with nothing
is doing this— show stg track. Pretending
around!   Tell

og duty - *lut*

vowels in wood

in trees w/ se

. Go kart thro

. Dico Tattersall

London /stauk

r "Buried alive by love" we f
onths later In a Castle out
tary man" and my favorite

pumering out 10 music videos for cky ii
a year I felt I had enough experience to
eo for my favorite band "HiM". I had
ed out, I will fly out to Finland, get e
qvored up and talk them into letting me dire
before they found out I was only 21! so a
s went by and I got a message from the
valo" that we were going to be in LA at
time. They were mixing there album in studio
I was in Hollywood filming jackass shit so I to
a perfect opportunity, and I didn't give a
an advance from the record label. I said
will pay for the video and if you like it y
t" we shot the video for $77,000 at the
ng Juliette lewes and the shit went # 1 a mo
e UK. BMG suggested that I do the next 3 h
that. Note to self - taking a $77,000 risk wa
worth every penny!"

the next vid
of prauge fo
of all time "and

# THE 69 EYES VIDEO SHOOT LOS ANGELES AND PHILADELPHIA

I am flying to Los Angeles with the 69 eyes to film a scene at the rainbow room for the Lost boys. I can't help to notice everyone loooking at us!! I thin its frcking hilarious! picture these dudes prancing through the airport—

# LOST BOYS!

Not to mention the X-ray machine, Jussi seriously took 25 minutes taking off h punk rock flare to get through the termin the people behind him were so pissed! I hope missed theyre flights! Ha!

TL0304   GA      GA0  22      COMP

EVENT CODE      SECTION/AISLE   ROW/BOX  SEAT      ADMISSION

$   0.00   STANDING ROOM              0.00

ELECTRIC FACTORY PRESENTS

THE 69 EYES

AN ALL WEATHER EVENT

SECTION/AISLE

GA            THEATRE OF LIVING ARTS

TM    1X      334 SOUTH ST, PHILA.

ROW   SEAT

GA0  22      SAT MAR 4, 2006 9:00PM

TLA600C

4MAR06

# CARVER CITY
## NEW ALBUM!!!!!

dear bam,
we have sirius radio on our tv and my son has been
listlen to your show. just recently i tuned in to the
show and and i have to say i was qiuet apalled
an angry mother

They took Hu to the Dowtown
Dallas Jail for 12 hours miss
the show and the departure
the buses to Houston. I
to stay there to bail him
I show up to the Jail at
and they wouldnt rele
cause he is still too
I went back to the
waited till 8am for
on the hotel door. I
door naked lookin
with a bloody
girlfriend. The
Novak a ride
dropped me an
meet me. I
Novaks $50
got on t
philly ms
definitely
least

I NEED A F
I'LL BE A JUNN
IN FOUR YEARS!

I like to draw pictures of my neighbors on busses

Going to hell!

I gave $20,000 to boarderline the local sk8park in westchester which is fucking pointless because when I go there I cant even break a sweat skating cause every kid and soccer mom wants to talk, have an autograph or shoot a fucking photo and I dont mind it when im out, but NOT when Im skating. So i dont go there anymore. I built a fucking massive ramp in my backyard to skate for $100,000 to the fdr nesskins to build. Now the fucking township is trying to tear it down. because its a dangerous structure. No fucking shIt! I will skate this ramp till they physically come in with the bare hands and remove it. FUCK THEM OLD HORSE POETRY LOVING FAGGOTS!

Bam

on
w
Ramp ↓

SERIOUS
AS
SHITWATER!

RGERa

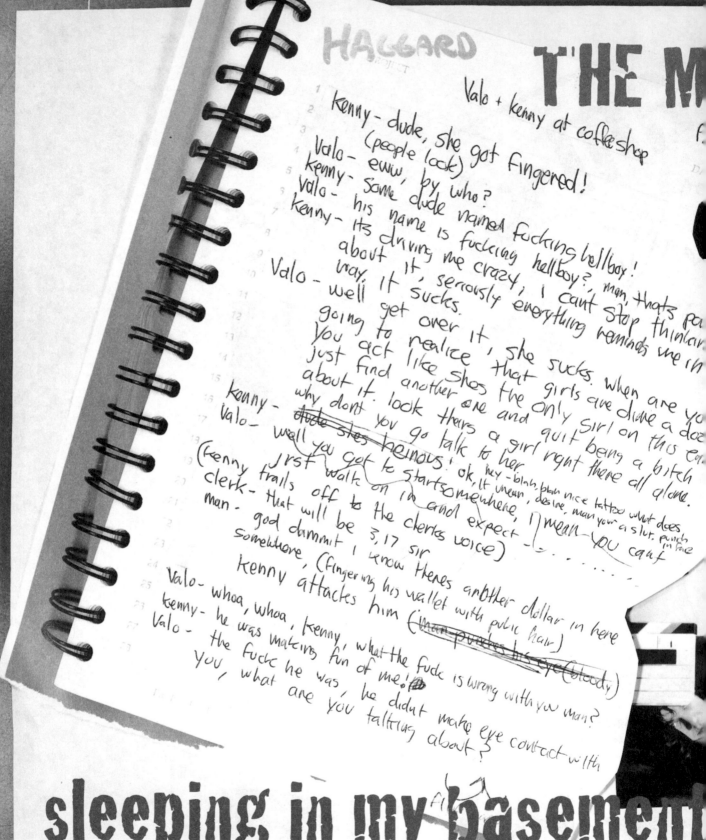

④

# during a take because
# iNg PROBleMS

Novak had a little too much fun
Being naked and not getting kick
ed out for once he flew to the
show in Orlando Florida to join
the tour with me for good. I
wanted to make his existance
worthy by taking a shit in the
middle of the street, but his diet
consists of booze, pills and cocaine
so he didnt have to shit till the
4th day of tour in Dallas Texas.
He says "Bam break out the camera I
have to shit." Of course I do and
He goes out into the middle of the
Freeway and drops trou! He Now
Has a foot of shit hangin out of
His ass causing a great traffic
Jam. The 3rd car that passed him beeped
and flicked him off, the fourth car was
A police car! a fucking police car!!
worst timing ever, he couldnt even hide
They come out instantly handcuffing
Him and walks up to me and say
"You think its fucking funny to
Film your pal shit in the middle
Of the street?" I bursted out
laughing and said "NO!"

Liquor and Poker

MAD LIBS
HOW TO SURVIVE
A SANDSTORM

CKY
www.cky-online.com

ALWAYS STRIKE A MATCH AWAY FROM YOU

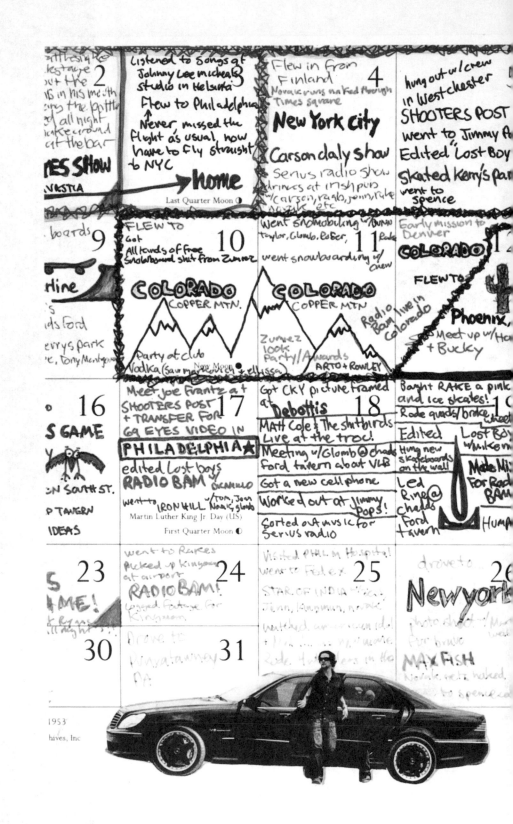

| | | | |
|---|---|---|---|
| ...ttleston... ...kestore... ...ut the... 16 in his mouth ...ing the bottle ...ed all night ...krecround ...at the bar **TES SHOW** ...NESTIA ...**2** | Listened to Songs at Johnny Lee micheals studio in Helsinki **3** Flew to Philadelphia ↑ Never missed the flight as usual, now have to fly straight to NYC →home Last Quarter Moon ☽ | Flew in from Finland **4** Novak runs naked through Times square **New York City** Carson daly show Serius radio show drinks at irish pub w/Carson, rake, john rule etc | hung out w/crew in Westchester **5** SHOOTERS POST Went to Jimmy A... Edited "Lost Boy Skated Kerry's par... went to spence |
| ...boards **9** ...line ...s ...ds Ford ...errys park ...e, Tony Montgom... | FLEW TO **10** Got All kinds of free snolaboard shit from Zumiez **COLORADO** COPPER MTN. Party at club Vodka (Saw may... New Moon ● | Went snowmobiling **11** taylor, Glomb, Raker went snowboarding w/ crew **COLORADO** COPPER MTN Zumiez 100k Party / Awards ARTO + ROWLEY | Early mission to Denver **12** **COLORADO** FLEW TO Phoenix, Radio Bam live in Colorado Meet up w/Ha... + Bucky |
| o **16** **S GAME** ...y N SOUTH ST. P TAVERN IDEAS | Meet joe Frantz a + **17** SHOOTERS POST + TRANSFER FOR 69 EYES VIDEO IN **PHILADELPHIA ★** edited Lost boys **RADIO BAM** w/DCAMILLO Went to IRON HILL w/Tom, Joan Noak, glomb Martin Luther King Jr Day (US) First Quarter Moon ◑ | Got CKY picture framed **18** at **Debottis** Matt Cole & The shitbirds Live at the troc! Meeting w/Glomb @ chads ford tavern about VLB Got a new cell phone Worked out at Jimmy Pops! Sorted out music for Serius radio | Bught RAKE a pink **19** and ice skates! Rode quads/broke... Edited Lost Boy w/Mike om... Hung new skateboards on the wall Led Ring @ chads ford tavern Made Mi... For Rad... BAM HUMP... |
| S **23** HME! k...y... ll night... | Went to Rakes **24** picked up Kingson at airport **RADIO BAM!** Logged footage for Kingman Drove to | Visited PHIL in Hospital **25** Went to Fo... ex STAR OF INDIA w/Bren Jenn, kingman, novak watched un... un idol + ... w... movie Rode 4 wheelers in the | drove to **26** **New york** photo shoot w/Mar... for brvie **MAX FISH** Novak gets naked ...to spence... |
| **30** | Drove to **31** Pinyatowney PA! | | |

1953
...y
hives, Inc

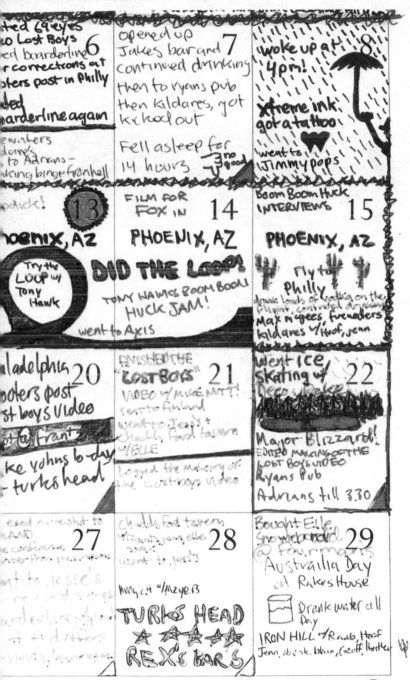

| | | |
|---|---|---|
| ...ted 69 eyes / ...o Lost Boys / ...ed boarderline / r corrections at / ...ters post in Philly / ...ed / ...arderline again / ...e waters / ...dane's / ...to Adrians- / ...king binge frankhell **6** | opened up / Jakes bar and / continued drinking / then to ryans pub / then kildares, got / kicked out / Fell asleep for / 14 hours ~ 3 no good **7** | woke up at / 4pm! / xtreme ink / got a tattoo ♥ / went to / Jimmy pops **8** |
| ...dvicle! **13** / ...oenix, AZ / Try the / LOOP w/ / Tony / Hawk | FILM FOR / FOX in **14** / PHOENIX, AZ / DID THE LOOP! / TONY HAWKS BOOM BOOM / HUCK JAM! / went to Axis | Boom Boom Huck / INTERVIEWS **15** / PHOENIX, AZ / fly to / Philly / drank loads of vodka on the / flight, continued drinking / Max mcgees, fire waters / kildares w/Hoof, jenn |
| ...iladelphia **20** / ...oters post / ...st boys video / ...ta Frant / ...ke yohns to day / -turks head | FINISHED THE / "LOST BOYS" **21** / VIDEO w/ MIKE NUTT! / sent to finland / went to Jean's + / chadds Ford tavern / w/ELLE / Logged the Making of / the "Lost boys video | went ICE / skating w/ **22** / Deco water / Major Blizzard! / EDITED MAKING OF THE / LOST BOYS VIDEO / Ryans pub / Adrians till 3.30 |
| ...exed ...e shit to / ...AND **27** / ...e conference / ...ner from the... / ...nt to Jesse's / ...re...d's ones / ...ardeatline...hy... / ...t ti drifters / ...rants, hanna.... | chadds Ford tavern / w/Frants, jenn, elle / no axis / went to jess's / Amy out w/meyers **28** / TURKS HEAD / ⭐⭐⭐⭐⭐ / REX'S BAR'S | Bought Elle / snowboard **29** / @ Fourman's / Australlia Day / at Rakes House / 🥃 Drank water all / Day / IRON HILL w/Raab, Hoof / Jenn, iben.k, blain, Geoff, Heather |

ARGERA
GEE PHOTO 2000'

BAM 18.11

| 14 | 15 | 16 | 17 |
|---|---|---|---|
| Ben Gravends! skated FDR interview w/ vito | 4 wheel version at the pine barrens in New Jersey! SHIT GOOSE! went to Jimmy Pops wired for shibo | Got 6 pictures framed at debaties in west chester skated empty pool in PA went to 15N w/ crew | Flew to HOLLYWOOD PI restaurant meetings w/ terry |

| 21 | 22 | 23 | 24 |
|---|---|---|---|
| edited shit took a limo to Philly w/ the girls Hung out with Hillary Diff in Philly Mebe Turks head inn | built ramp into the pool! shot photos! skated boardline w/ mike macdonald got a shower!!! Noticed chicks in pool! | film Rockstars episode! Jimmy pop freestyle too! Tim vito pawl BLOODHOUND GANGS FIRST SHOW | FILMED ROCKSTAR EPISODE |

element

T BRICKS ON THE GAS PEDALS TO SEE

KATE TRICK, AND THAT SHIT IS A

RNSWALLOWERS!

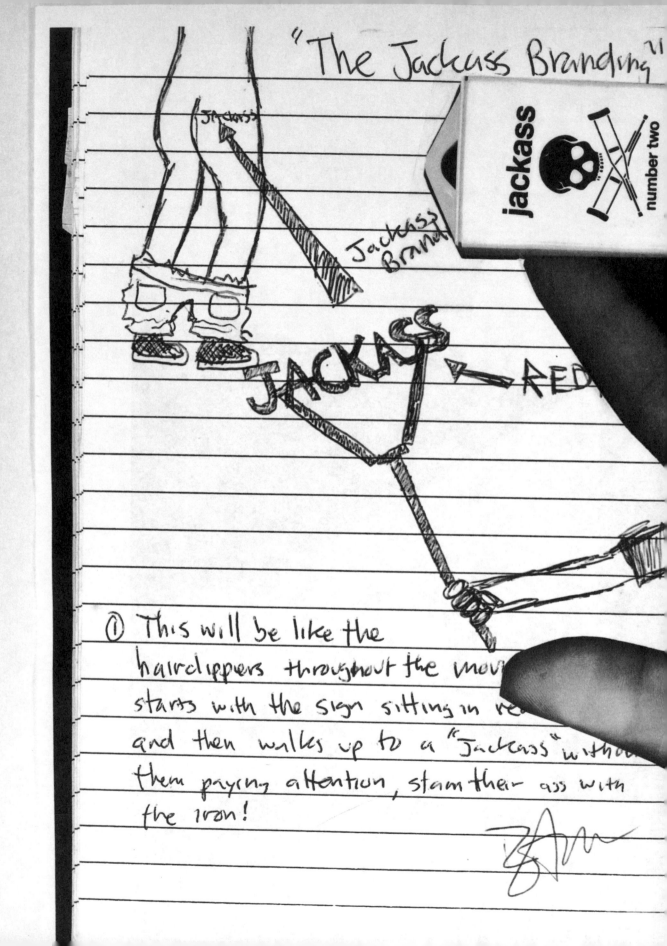

"The Jackass Branding"

jackass
number two

Jackass

Jackass
Brand

JACKASS ← RED

① This will be like the
hairclippers throughout the mov
starts with the sign sitting in re
and then walks up to a "Jackass" witho
them paying attention, stam their ass with
the iron!

RANDOM IDEAS

takes a s___ asshit a
off- mass___ fireworks

"Jackass ___randing.

___ and ___ their ro
___ in all the
___ or thier a

___ house l

___ to you

I Agreed to get a ___
branding of a skull and cross ___
bones for Jackass 2, when it was
time to film the bit in miami it was
wasnt what we had discussed. it was
a mini hard dick! i said "jeff what
the fuck?. i didnt agree to this! He
said "look at the contract you signed,
u agreed to get a branding, it didnt
say of what it just says a branding in
general, your stuck with this, this is
your Bit. so now I have an infected
dick farm on my ass! Forever.
thank god for those bandaids!

Sterility
guaranteed
unless package
damaged or
open.

...co announces
...a Top Hat
...h black & white
...ped circus
...ut!

OBJECT-
HIT SOMEONES DICK AGAINST THIER
WILL!

100
90
80
70
60
50
40
30
20
10

HIT
ME

STEP
RIGHT
UP

WELCOME

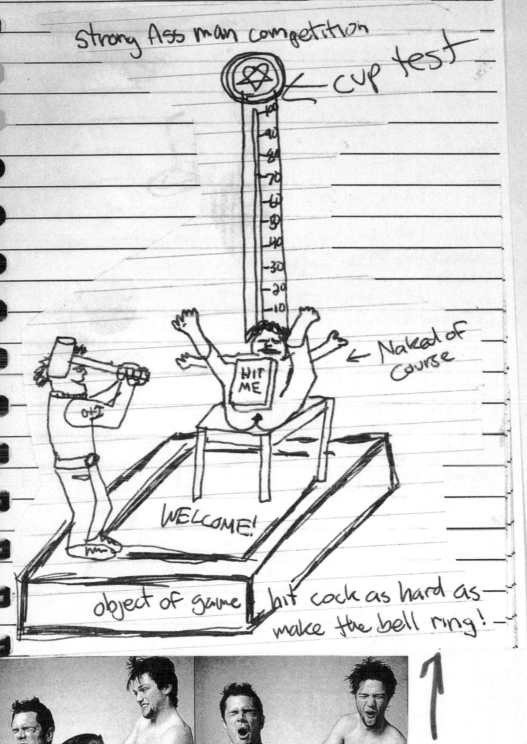

strong Ass man competition

cup test →

100
90
80
70
60
50
40
30
20
10

← Naked of course

HIT ME

OUT

WELCOME!

object of game: hit cock as hard as make the bell ring!

NEW IDEAS

LOGGED HIM TAPES
TILL 3pm       **3**
drove Lambo w/ shitgoose
Got Haircut
EDITED HIM DOC.

DVffers II
Daylight Saving Time begins

**drank**
**Booze**
Novak did a naked pirr to Kokle
**Radio Bam**

Skated the
Driveway

Cops came over
thanks to jenn
and me! (Bam) **10**

Slept
the day
away

Filmed vito
For cky challenge **11**

went to jess's in lambo
Mitch's gym
**RADIO BAM**
Mitch's gym again
HOOTERS

**12**
NEW. YORK
TRL
autograph sig.
Virgin megastore

**17**
Fly to
California

**18**
Jackass
Commentary

went to Roxy w/ Bam
+ Jessica simpson

**19**
Jackass
Commentary

**24**          **25**          **26**

EDITED @ Dakota
VH1 interview **1**

# HIM
## MANSION!

April Fool's Day
Last Quarter Moon ◐

LOS ANGEL
TO PHILADE
LOGGED HIM F
MITCH'S GYM
FAIR
ELEMENT
AUTOGR
SIGNIA

GOT ANNIHILA
KILDARES vs J
pooltable ✝✝
New
TURBONE
sk8
FDR
Goosecre
Visited Jess
Hooters, 15 v

ne barrens
## New Jersey

Shoot w/
**mark weiss** **7**

meeting w/ cartoon
People at kildares

ERVIEW w/ BRAND

Skated the driveway **8**

Billy Idol in
**Philadelphia**

Manayunk w/ Jimmy Pop
New Moon ●

*life is a flying leap*

film
HIM

Fanna ge
the
Stay " ssc

2

27

always told my self when I turn 21 I wont be that
that goes straight to the bar, sure enough my 21s
day I was at 15 north Hammering down shots! I've wasted many
y nights at the bar talking to randoms about absolutely noth
thinking it was so cool getting recognized by Hot chicks. I w
ould have rewound life and skated 50% of my alchohol consu
d, Dont get me wrong Im all for getting shitfaced, but when
do it everynight for 2 years you got to take a step b
chill. The problem with me is that I could never say
only drink on special occasions because everynight is a
cial occasion. One night I will be at kildares with the C
, then to the troc for a children of bodom show, then to LA
Sean Penn and John cusack on the beach. Every fucking
is a special occasion, thats the problem. But
least its a good Problem.

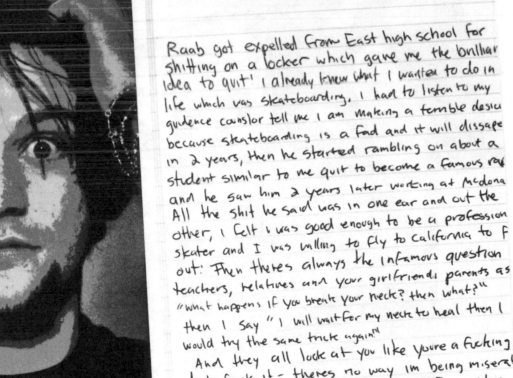

Raab got expelled from East high school for
shitting on a locker which gave me the brilliar
idea to quit! I already knew what I wanted to do in
life which was skateboarding. I had to listen to my
guidence counslor tell me I am making a terrible desu
because skateboarding is a fad and it will dissape
in 2 years, then he started rambling on about a
student similar to me quit to become a famous ra
and he saw him 2 years later working at Mcdona
All the shit he said was in one ear and out the
other, I felt I was good enough to be a profession
skater and I was willing to fly to california to f
out. Then theres always the infamous question
teachers, relatives and your girlfriends parents as
"what happens if you break your neck? then what?"
then I say "I will wait for my neck to heal then I
would try the same trick again"

   And they all look at you like youre a fucking
idiot. fuck it – theres no way im being misera
like all of you people working a 9 to 5 everyday.

   I will take my chances!

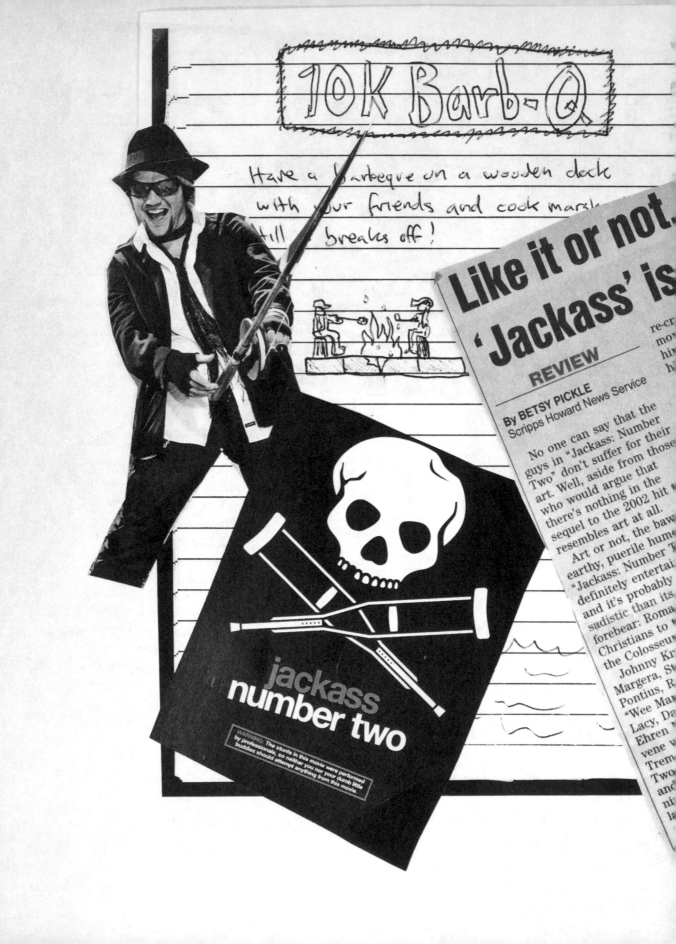

**...ck**

...Tom & Jerry"
...lindfolding
...subjecting
...a yak's caresses.
...quence has a
...bulls keeping an
...Margera as he
...his buttocks to be
...led.
...her animals contribut-
...to the pain and *suffer-*
...*ing* include sharks, ana-
...ondas, a king cobra, a
...leech, bees and a stallion.
    The group's fascination
with bodily emissions hits
its peak (or *nadir*) with
the stallion. It's the one
part of the film that
requires a black censoring
bar.

    What makes all this
watchable is the gleeful
attitude and friendship o...
the men, and the fact tha...
even the most disgusting
antics are amusing,
whether in a "laughing ...
with them" or "laughing ...
them" spirit.

    There's no order to the...
antics, and Tremaine
could have done a better
job of editing some of the...
weaker material and orga...
nizing more of a build. At...
95 minutes, the film
should never drag, but it
does a couple of times.
    Rated R for extremely
crude and dangerous
stunts, sexual content,
nudity and language.

...3am
...ris
..., Jason
..., Preston
...nd and
...y recon-
...ctor Jeff
..."Number
...he first film
...-of-the-millen-
...show that
...t, excrement,
...and an obsession
...turing the male
...r abound in "Two."
...film starts, hilari-
...bulls — through a sub-
...an neighborhood, with
...e huffing, overgrown
...oys barely staying ahead
...of them. Later, Knoxville

We put a $10 right out front of a supermarket with shit underneath and film what idiot picks it up. Bam-Bam come out of nowhere in nice suits like News reporters. with a mic and the whole deal. "congradulations you are the winner of the shit dollar, how do you feel? are you gonna buy a lot of shit with that dollar sir? give him a ghetto trophy.

115

To think, 10 minutes after this photo was taken Knoxville was in the hospital for a concusion cause dunn drove over a Mountain Lion!

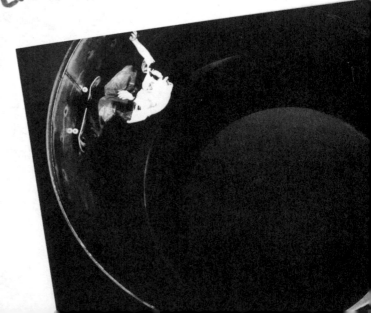

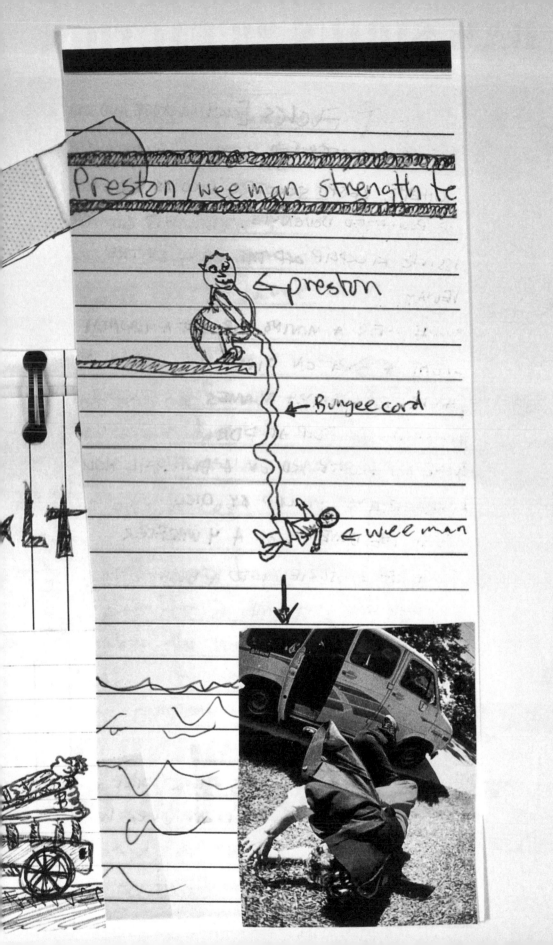

**Preston/weeman strength te**

←preston

← Bungee cord

←weeman

ME AND KNOXVILLE FUCKING
AROUND ON BIKES AT THE
PARAMOUNT LOT 2 WEEKS
BEFORE HE FUCKED HIS
DICK UP TRYING TO BACK
FLIP ON A DIRT BIKE ..

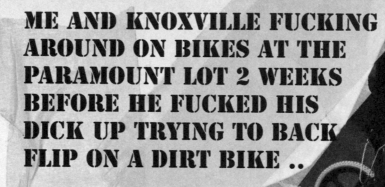

MISSY & MYSELF
KISSING MAJA OF
THE SOUNDS BEFORE
HER SHOW AT THE
PALLADIUM .....

IGGY AND I DRUNK AT A MYS

# SUNSET MARQUIS
## MISSION
## LOS
## ANGELES
## 08

Iggy Pop plays the wedding. Now im fuckin freinds with him and will meet him with some booze before one of his shows! fuck you if you have something to say!

**CE INTERVIEW**

BAM MARGERA • TRICK TIPS • JASON DILL

411 BAM.

PARENTAL ADVISORY EXPLICIT CONTENT

FREE BAM BONUS DVD!

the bam issue
profile, road trip, spot check, and more

jason dill
day in the life

hot wheels
arms on fire

61

411 video magazine    skateboarding

2005

2005

May there be silly nights like this one

live late lasting laughs ..........

TH

28  FLY TO Finland

Begin Filming Ville's Making of the album for SIRE!

DRINKS AT THE SCANDIC
w/ 69 eyes, Burton, Mige, Ville, Jonna, Gas, Etc

29  Hellzinki, FINLAND

FILMED 16mm w/ crane at TORNI

Lost and Found w/ Ville, Jenn, Jonna, Mige, + The 69-eyes

Hel FI

Drinks
CIGARE
BAR LOO
LOST AN
JOHNNY
Edited
Video L
skated
Color co
Shooter
Skated
Boar

...stage
...t the
...s in his mouth
...y the bottle
...d all night
...e crowd
...t the bar

...ES SHOW

...VISTLA

2  Listened to songs at Johnny Lee michael's studio in Helsinki

Flew to Philadelphia
↳ Never missed the flight as usual!
have ...
to NYC

4  Flew in from Finland
Moravic runs naked through Times square
New York City
...ily show

5  hung out w/ crew in Westchester
SHOOTERS POST
went to Jimmy Pops
Edited "Lost Boys"

...boards 9
FLEW
Got
All kinds o
Snowboar...

...tine

CO...

...ts ford

...rry's park
...c, Tony Montyom...

Party a
Vodka (S...

16  Meet J
SHOOTE...
+ TRANS
69 EY...
...S GAME

PHIL...

THEE HOBBIT HOLE

# JANUARY

RATTLESNAKE BOOZE

30

Helzinki,
**FINLAND**
woke up at 2pm
**HIM SHOW**
At TAVASTIA KLUB

Drink Backstage till 4am

Kabuki restaurant

Helzinki,
**FINLAND**
**HIM SHOW**
At TAVASTIA KLUB

1

Drink Backstage till 4am

New Year's Day

6

Opened up
Jakes bar and 7
continued drinking
then to ryans pub
then kildares, got
kicked out

Fell asleep for
14 hours  3 no good

woke up at 8
4pm!

Xtreme ink,
got a tattoo

went to
Jimmy pops

MAD HOUSE

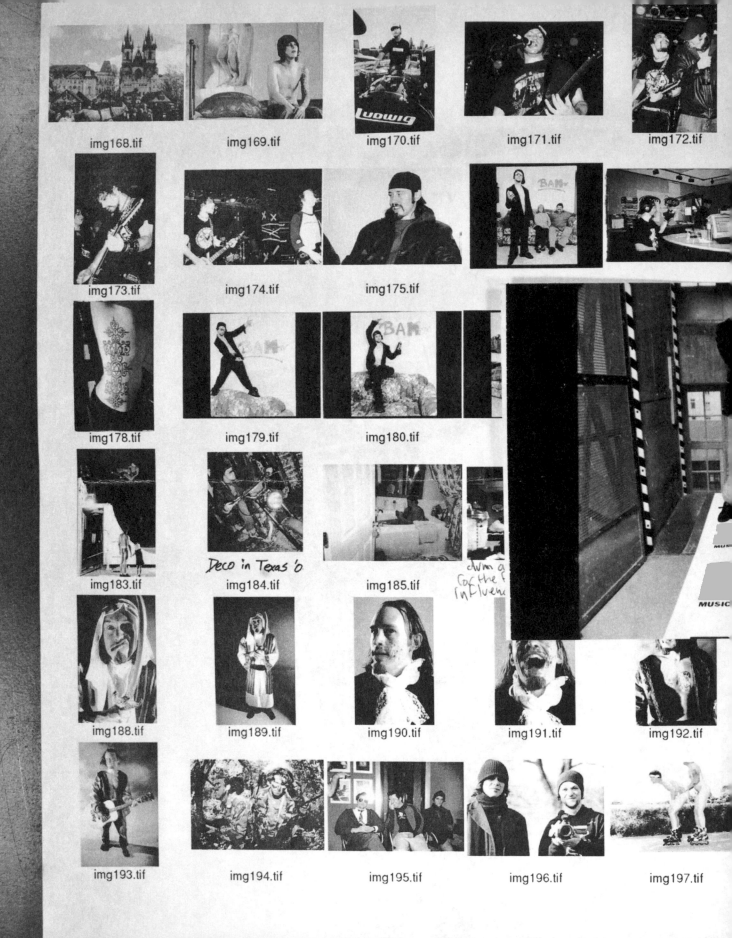

img168.tif  img169.tif  img170.tif  img171.tif  img172.tif

img173.tif  img174.tif  img175.tif

img178.tif  img179.tif  img180.tif

img183.tif  img184.tif  img185.tif

Deco in Texas '0

img188.tif  img189.tif  img190.tif  img191.tif  img192.tif

img193.tif  img194.tif  img195.tif  img196.tif  img197.tif

img107.tif

img108.tif

img109.tif img110.tif

gay fags is the funniest skit I think I have ever
filmed, as far as im concerned this is my best
work, 2 fags on rollerblade humping eachotter
damn brilliant!

Bamboozled!

img111.tif

img114.tif

img115.tif

img116.tif

img119.tif

img120.tif

img121.tif

img124.tif

img125.tif

img126.tif

img127.tif

img128.tif

Gaudenzia

img129.tif

img130.tif

img131.tif

img132.tif

img133.tif

Gaudenzia

img134.tif

img135.tif

img137.tif

phil drove this piece of shit
for 3½ years, there was a hole in the floor
and exaust leaked up in the car for us to breathe, this car is

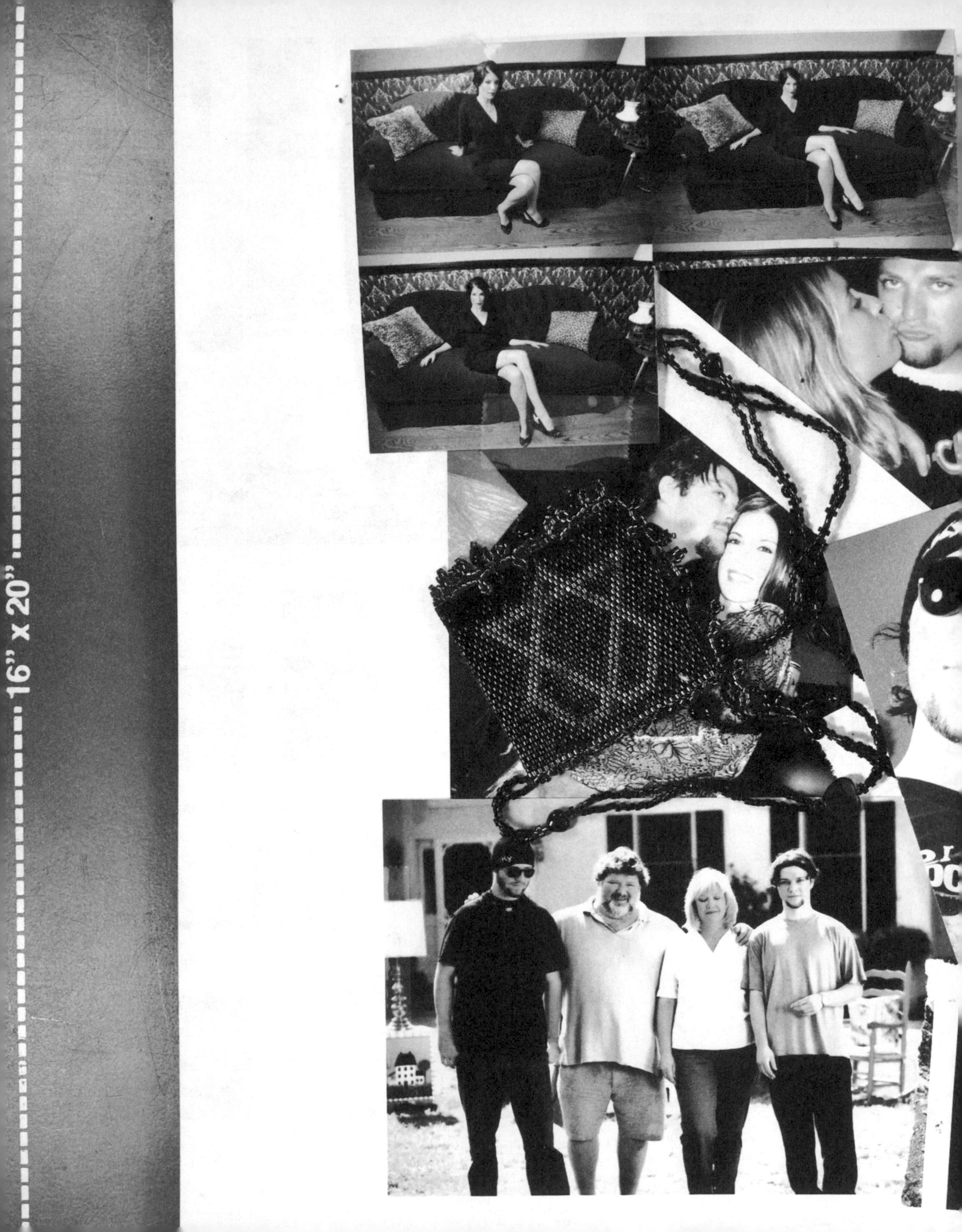
16" x 20"

Take your beer
See who your
Sex with!
Have A !@%$# Day.
Mike Vallely
DANG!

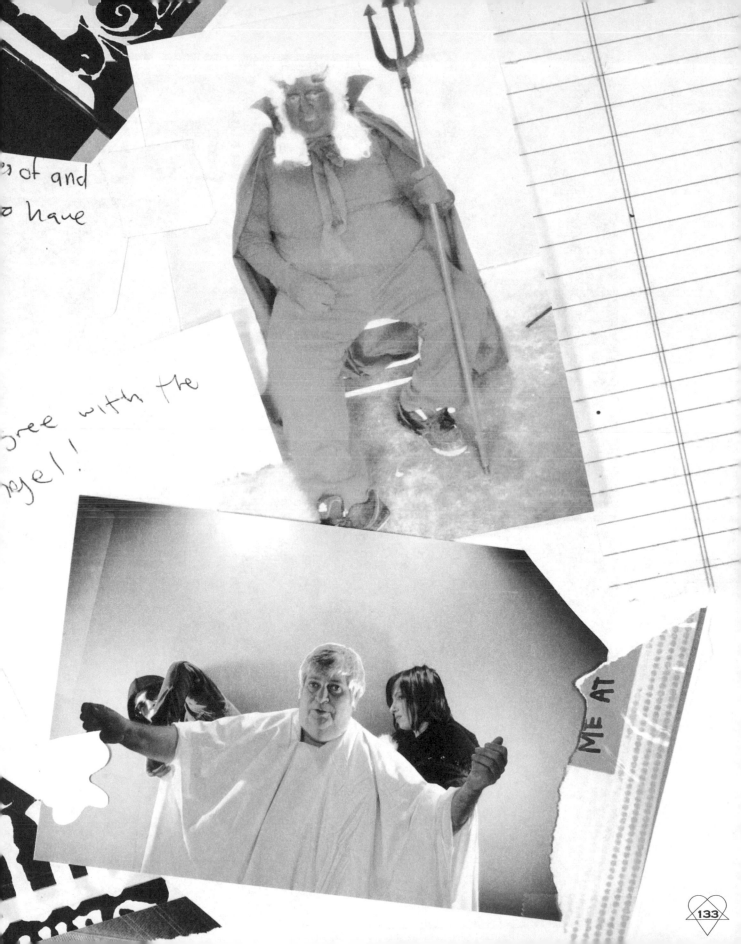

s of and
o have

free with the
ngel!!

ME AT

133

Baby shambles

ident that
process
iciently

e primary elections in May.
County Commissioner
arol Aichele said the pres-
nce of two new voting sys-
ms caused the totaling of
otes after the primary elec-
ons to take until the morn-
g after polls closed – much
ter than usual.
The county's 223 precincts
ad to have officials bring
heir pape         s to the
hester           artment
f Vote            n West
   h              d after

Brandon "Bam" Margera h
order from his ex-girlfriend
vell broke into his Pocops

Page A2

committe
e budg

quickly,
ve that
ot a day

# Margera files for protection

**By BRIAN FANELLI**
Staff Writer

WEST CHESTER – The ongoing turmoil between local celebrity Brandon "Bam" Margera and his ex-girlfriend, Jennifer Rivell, continued on Friday, as Margera appeared in a Chester County Common Pleas Court for a protection from abuse (PFA) hearing, after Rivell allegedly broke into his Pocopson residence a few weeks ago.

Margera, who turned

September, appeared be Common Pleas Court Ju Paula Francisco Ott dres in black boots splatte with white paint, a black coat and black pants. A waited to take the stand held the hand of his fian Missy Rothstein.

The star of MTV's "Viv Bam" and "Jackass" test that Rivell, 33, climbed wall surrounding his idence, entered the and kicked in a or on Oct. 17.

RGERA, Pag

Staff photo by Tom Kelly IV
for a protection from abuse
er Rivell. Margera claims Ri
ence a few weeks ago.

s, v
fles

## INSIDE TODAY

| | |
|---|---|
| siness | B1 |
| ster County | A3 |
| and gasified | D1 |
| glass pu | B4,5 |
| | A4 |
| | A2 |
| | B3 |
| | A5 |
| | C1 |
| | B3 |
| | B6 |

Ellis

The Rubinstein's of
store's branch in Ken
re celebrates 25 year
ness. The store has
three locations in its
century of business.

See Br

AY
s the Penns
lastic Athletic
oss country me
Area runners
al threats.

8  715

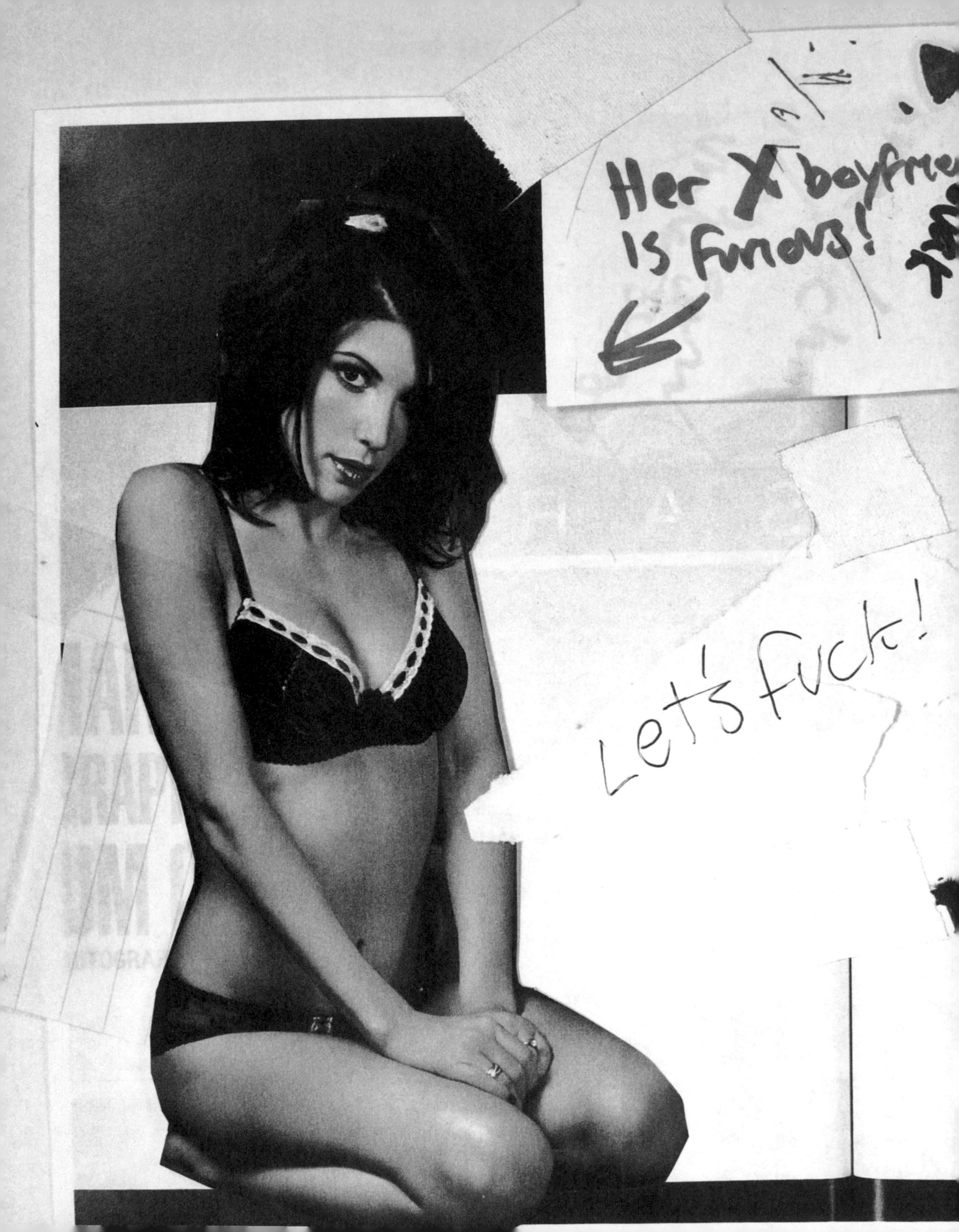
Her X boyfrie
is furious!
Let's fuck!

# AN UNHOLY U...
## BAM MARGERA FACES DOWN THE FINAL FRONTI...

...people laugh you know...

...ish teacher says "you idolize tha...
he does nothing for society, hes a...
real life!" i do nothing for society...
aske that to the 19 million motherfuc...
laughing at the dickfarm on my a...
you think andre agassi does shit f...
or pete fagit ass rose? yes they...
they hit a ball and run, andpush a...
around, thats the only differen...
i didn't get to...

10. Nouales sirlfr...

11. i like what th...
    skateboard...
    i drove...
    and...
    fuck...

12. It...

13. INT. 1...
    2. D...
    3. Jes...
    4. Du...
    5. J.M...

we stupid ass

ckass!?
ckass in
y dont you
s on the floor
g it!
e society?
ertain?
e of wood
t least
fare ahhahe

d on

Both!!!
put it
on paper

It's a cold morning in early January in West Chester, Pa. Bam Margera and a film crew are outside a cigar shop, filming scenes for his new MTV reality show, *Bam's Unholy Union*, which follows the exploits of the Jackass star and his bride-to-be, Melissa "Missy" Rothstein as they prepare to join in wedded bliss.

check her ass↓ 2·17·07

Probably fucked 10mins later→

# DUBAI

Just landed in Dubai after a draining 17 hour flight. Now I don't know why they chose us to pick on but Missy and I both had to strip nude and checked our asses for drugs. I know perez hilton put a photo of us on the website that we were coming here for a honeymoon, and that music producer just got in big trouble for having coke on him. so they said "don't bring any drugs" haha. So maybe that. Or the fact that we said we were married which is true. But it said Rothstien and Magera.

Meanwhile im wearing a rosary and Missy is a jew. They must have just thought we were up to no good. So 3hrs later of total bullshit. Missy is ready to fly home and I made her power it out to the resort. Once we got there it was totally 5ive. We offically got fucked

I Told you I Frenched her, but I Fucked

BAMS HOO

er !

| 7 | 8 | 9 | 10 | 11 | 12 | 13 |
| 14 | 15 | 16 | 17 | 18 | 19 | 20 |
| 21 | 22 | 23 | 24 | 25 | 26 | 27 |
| 28 | 29 | 30 | 31 | | | |

300 sit ups
Kickflip peppermill **4**

went to Bloodhound
Gang Barb-@

New Hope ✚

Saw the USED in wilmington
Party @ my house w/Used
and Jared Leto

Drove to wilmington for
skate spots **11**

King of prussia mall
Look for skatespots
300 sit ups
saw
Billy IDOL in A.C.

stayed at
Grandparents' Day (US)

Missy's beachouse @NJ
First Quarter Moon ●
300 SIT UPS

**INTERVIEWS**
**w/MTV2** **18**

TONY HAWK DEMO
ATHENS,
GEORGIA!

DINNER @ TRANSMETRO
DRIVE TO ATLANTA w/mikev

**25**

LA

ZEIT

I drink beer an
missy doesnt dri
weed which is th
why the fuck do
X girlfriend was exa
s fun, but after
in flames, Mn
opposites attract

I knew this bitch was the one

Hockey kicks ass. Bam and Brandon. Above, Phil and Bam.

MISSY B-DAY at Rock 'n Ring

w.knm/Beatstom
Billy talent
Mond S

HOTEL DE ROME
BERLIN

1. Drink w/ panda cow
2. The search for duscon mandlite
3. Missy X flips out / caught on film
   servaillence freaks out. we arro
   him
4. Antique car
5. Novak winds up in jail
6. court for 6 tickets
7. get in shape to kick 2's
8. element creatve meetings
9. designing adio shoes
10. meeting carte for New shit
11. skate at tony hawkes
    see the grand canyon
12. Jessicas shit in the pool.

⬠

Behren
Tel +4
mail info.derom
hotels.qom
rrows
Rcar and
1000 Bricks
ave on

anthon

during INT.

outdo yourself, do
No Like jackass
beat that bit
and did what
ten times better.

ger shop break glass on wedding phone
t barn sledge hammer your door in?)
ative juice,
Noose hung!
/ we save money!
ment, 400,000 gone, 5,000 left
back! Just do it! ✓ 
Missy / who is your favorite
Band?

"I feel like im watching a porno,
only im in it."

# For once, leap

**W**est Chester, most proud county seat for Chester County has a juicy role — well, the borough's a full-fledged costar — in *Bam's Unholy Union*, an MTV reality series that will chronicle the no-doubt-arduous yet butterflies-in-the-tummy-thrilling preparations for the wedding of East High School drop-out and proud *Jackass* jackass **Bam Margera**, 27, and childhood sweetie **Missy Rothstein**, 26. (The show was to debut last night.)

Bam and Missy, who appeared on **Howard**

# is not a stunt

**Stern**'s Sirius show yesterday, say they're totally ready to keep married life as adventurous as possible by developing a technique to, um, consummate their holy bond while *driving*. (Missy conceded the couple's Hummer has wide seats.)

Radar Online reports that Bam, whose latest sub-Mensa movie, *Jackass Number Two*, has grossed $84.5 mil, won't sell out his roots to move to New York or Lalaland. "Everything I need is in Pennsylvania," he tells the New York Daily News. Rock on, Skateboard Dude!

The day before the wedd
the new ramp with Ton
death gap for the first
it and try forcing no
barges it after a heavy n
in the middle and bre
dipshit gets rushed to th
perscuption to percocettes. N
wheel chair going down
20 that day. 20! then
days later and start

we had a hesh sesh on
ck. We were trying the
e. Tony and I both make
to be the third. He
of boozing and jumps off
both of his feet. The
itall gets 2 casts and a
es in the wedding in a
aisle pilled up. He ate all
vent to baltimore a few
hooting heroin again!

## Bam & Missy TIE THE KNOT!

*Jackass* star and pro-skater **Brandon "Bam" Margera**, 27, and graphic designer Melissa "Missy" Rothstein, 26, married before 350 guests including skating legend **Tony Hawk** and rocker **Iggy Pop** in Philadelphia on Feb. 3! The wedding, which aired April 3 on MTV's *Bam's Unholy Union*, capped off a madcap romance: The couple may have known each other since the sixth grade but only started dating two years ago. Last year, Bam popped the question outside of Cartier at the King of Prussia Mall in Pennsylvania. "Missy's totally down with Bam's craziness and supports him," MTV ...okesman Travis Hicks tells *Star*. "They al-...s seem like th...... ....n."

...PPEL ★

| | | |
|---|---|---|
| | **Civic Holiday** (CAN except Quebec) | Edited HIM do... / bashed in Missy's sisters door |
| went to **50 cents** house in connecticut | **8** rove Hummer from Port Jervis to New Hope / Cribs @ evil Jareds cracked head open 12 staples in Head | **9** meeting w/ bran, Fr... terry about animatio... **New Hope** w/ Terry, Frantz, miss... Ape + Phil bought candelabras / Radio Bam |
| **14** RODE BIKE TO DELAWARE / GOSE CREEK GRILL Iked 7 miles / atched VLB @ duffers / +W SKELETON KEY | **15** RODE BIKE TO W.C. / SOLD CLOTHES IN DELAWARE / Rode bike w/shutthords / RADIO BAM / Firewaters/kildares Blarney stone | **16** Rode bike / 40 laps in pool / Jimmy pops / Saw Wed d.w.o Cheale / Blarney w/Jen.J kildares/My hous... |
| **21** ash ummer / JIT HIM DOC / OOTERS / "red eye" w/Missy Novak / J sit ups | **22** BAHAMAS | **23** |
| **28** MTV AWARDS | **29** FLY HOME to ... chester | **30** Fairmans to Fox, shit / EDIT HIM Darklight MOA... |

← The beam of Jim!

I just got off the philly flight to denver and the first dude I see is glomb. He hands me the phone and insists I talk to brett micheals from poison to get vain of jenna on the Poisoned Tour. Brett answe and asks how im doing. I said "Tell you the truth not very well im going to a rehab in Arizona. He said "which one"? I said "Sierra tus Hes told me he has been there and its not for me, I will be doing group activities lil puzzles and water volleyball. and i'd be bet off renting a harley, drive across country and clear my head. I took his advice only I rented a shitty chevrolet insted

F-REHAB!

Shitbagged in budapest 05

I order stella artois with

Knowledge of bars - a packed night club yo the dancefloor and n the heat of the mom saver!

kitty bit me!↓

7 minutes after this taken photo I was outside
Iron hill with a Zodker Coke peeing on the
window. suppose im not invited back?
I spilled my drink!

s of ice!

F $1.50

red out if your
non chelantly pis
nows cause their
cing. Brilliant tim

long beach tradeshow — passed out in
front of hotel door and left Tim o'connor
and noof on the sidewalk. And left my
wallet at the reception! Tim called my
Mom and said I was missing. She called
the cops!

soar

inal

CKY
THE LATEST GRE

Black/Slate                    Black/Royal

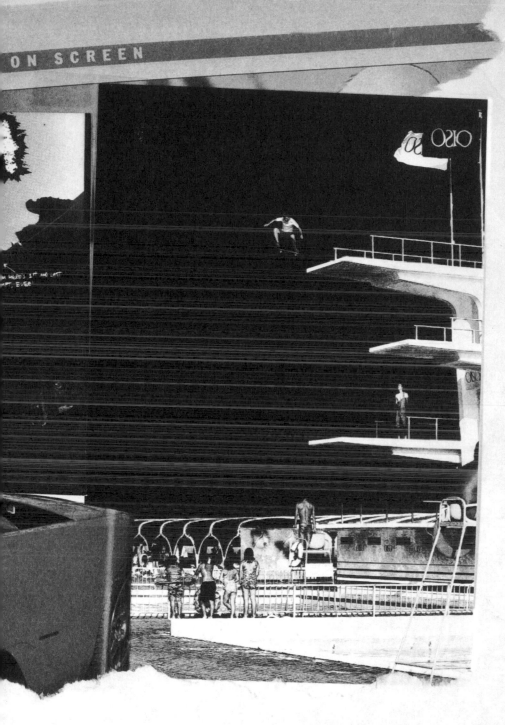

at kind of shit are you trying to pull? You got cut
f just when that guy was going to fuck that slut
tch. The music started to play just as that guy put
 the rubber. I thought you could do and say anything
  satellite radio? WHAT THE FUCK!!!!????? I HOPE I
DN'T GET ROBBED BY THIS FUCKING SIRIUS SATELLITE
CKING RADIO!!

ILL A FAN....KEEP UP THE GOOD WORK.

Im Sure at this point a lot of people must ha
and thought I was Some spoiled brat ass kid
driving around Some hot shit Ferrari that my
would like to give these people a News flash
~~reality check~~ ACROSS THE STREET FROM A SHIT FA
sharing a bedroom with my brother and
regal that my aunt Boof gave me for
from a fuckin row house In Linwood, P
in jail! So if you happen to be one of
Something to say about the ferra

MENSIO

11

...ked at me
...a rich family
...ought me, I
...ick — I LIVED
...FOR 20 years
...lly got a buick
...My relatives come
...half of them are
...cks who had
...at my fuck!

Love,
BAM!

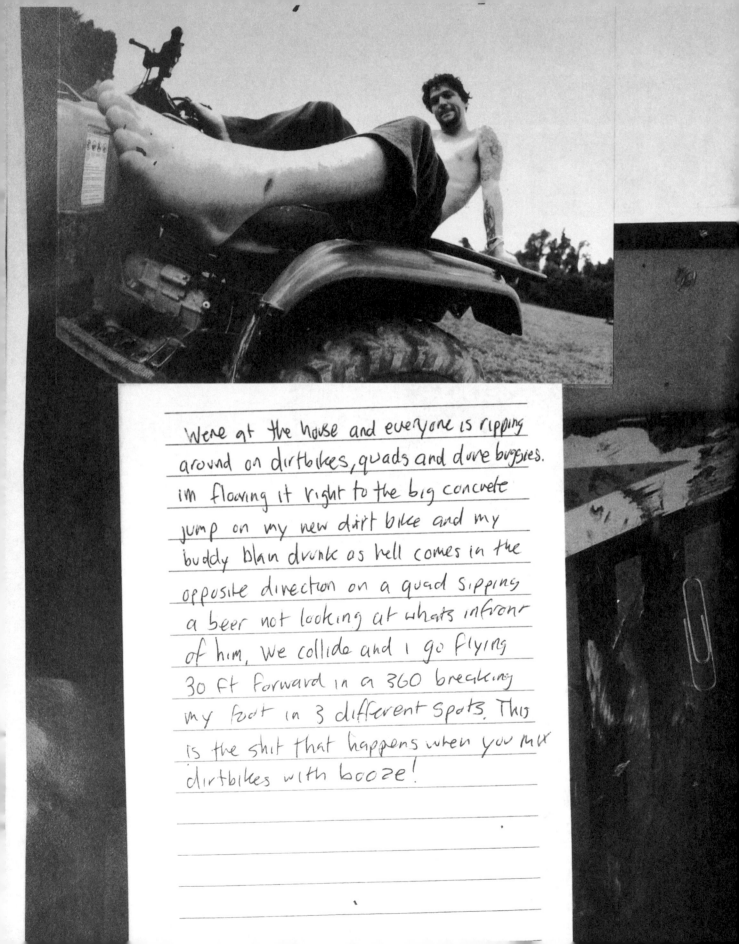

We're at the house and everyone is ripping around on dirtbikes, quads and dune buggies. im flooring it right to the big concrete jump on my new dirt bike and my buddy blain drunk as hell comes in the opposite direction on a quad sipping a beer not looking at whats infront of him, we collide and i go flying 30 ft forward in a 360 breaking my foot in 3 different spots. This is the shit that happens when you mix dirtbikes with booze!

This is the day I get slapped awake
by a strange film crew at 9am telling me
I have to film CRIBS now. I tell them to
comeback tommorow, they say we came here
from NYC and you have to film this. So I
now get up, fix myself a beer and t...
to get through this mess I got in! The
69 eyes show up as I am showing the hou...
I get the bright idea to wake up nov...
with Hot wax from a giant candle, I d...
so, then force him to go on the rope sw...
in the nude for cribs, once he agrees I
throw his sweatpants in the fire burn...
only the penis area out of the sweatpant...
now he is helping me show the new lamborg...
off with his dick hanging out. Best cr...
ever!

are, thats why you can buy it at fuckin

nothing i get in return for playing you th

27. pharrell williams "if you dont respect

be one!" VINCE NIEL K

28. fuck dave matthews, fuck vince neil,

of 3 stories breaking both of his le

about at 50 Rockin and/or rollin

28. Bucky lasek, Hawk, penny, tom bo

29. PINK (cheapskates) LOVES HEART

30. Dont ask me about jessica simp

that name your camera is going

31. Talent, noticed Dico/Miller, told

32. how did jackass happen?

33. drop in with Raccoon suit or a pair

34. why is jackass so gay? no pants is

35. sieze the day (ville in limo) show n

36. Meeting jimmy por shopping carts (Ro

37. VLB highlights (working with a crew of

1. Europe

2. delasho/dannyway

3. state of bam

4. dont feed phil (Turbo)

5. Brazil helicopter

why do you fuck with

starbucks theres
POISON GIRL
macoy fell off
one more
made
tattoo
Milk

The township is trying to tear down my new ramp because they say someone might fall on it. No fuckin shit! i fall on it every time i skate it! thats the whole point of skateboarding is to do as many tricks as you can till you fall Mara

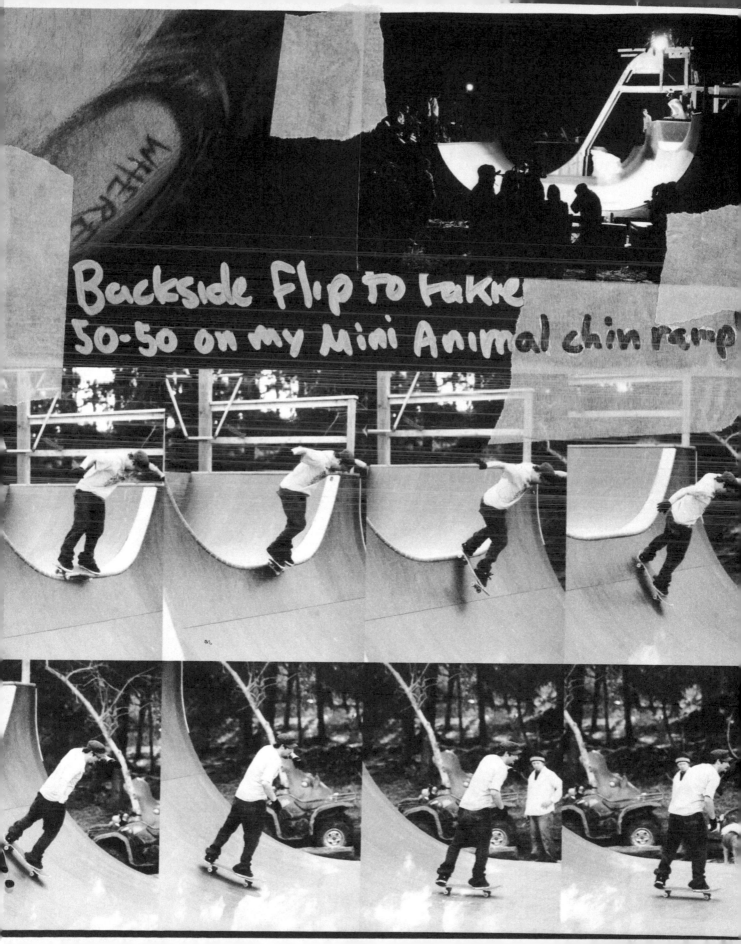

Backside Flip to fakie
50-50 on my Mini Animal chin ramp

TROUBLE

KITTY KITTY KITTY KITTY!

CATALUNYA
SHITBUM

MY
CATS →▲

MOUSEBREATH

MOUSEBREATH

←Tuna!

Meow Meow
Kitty Kitty
Meow Meow

Novak once again brings a college girl home to hump and I tried to put a stop to it so I had Seth paint a gay mural in his bedroom of a tom Sellek look alike toying with a cock! He came home and had to explain himself to the girl, but wound up laid anyway →

NOVAKS MURAL ABOVE HIS BED! AHAHAHA! →

"oh yeah, so hard, it feel
going to come out of m

Seth and i are sitting at the house bored to tears and nova went out to get some pussy at the bars. So Seth printed out a picture of tom selleck and painted a big mural of him sucking a dick about Novaks bed. Novak comes rolling in at 2am with a college chick. He turns on the lights and has to explain himself for 20 mintes B4 he got in her pants! AHAH

ike its
nouth"

HOTEL DE ROME

|  | | Price net | Deb ne |
|---|---|---|---|
| | ge | 1 | | |
| | nti | 1 | | |
| 03.01.06 | Communication Services VAT 22% | 1 | 1.66 | 1.66 |
| 03.01.06 | Telephone Charges VAT 22% | 1 | 172.00 | 172.00 |
| 03.01.06 | Telephone Charges VAT 22% | 1 | 9.51 | 9.51 |
| 03.01.06 | Telephone Charges VAT 22% | 1 | 28.69 | 28.69 |
| 03.01.06 | Telephone Charges VAT 22% | | 10.66 | 10.66 |
| 03.01.06 | Telep | | 3.06 | 3.06 |
| | | | 3.06 | |

that made a tent in his trousers, by putting some poo on a plate at a restaurant and complaining about it.

bastes and roasts himself. I get a terrible feeling. It's very scary. I have no earthly

wonderful at bathing parties...." Good, atmospheric stuff, and it gets

Telephone Charges VAT 22%    1
06    Accommodation Package
06    Communication Services VAT 22    1
.06    Telephone Charges VAT 22%
1.06    Telephone Charges VAT 22%
.01.06    Visa

Can take
shove them up her FU
until she starts wor
girls easily forget
dollar! if that
she would comp
6.04.2009!

Behrenstraß
Tel +49 30 4 6
E-mail info.derome@rocco

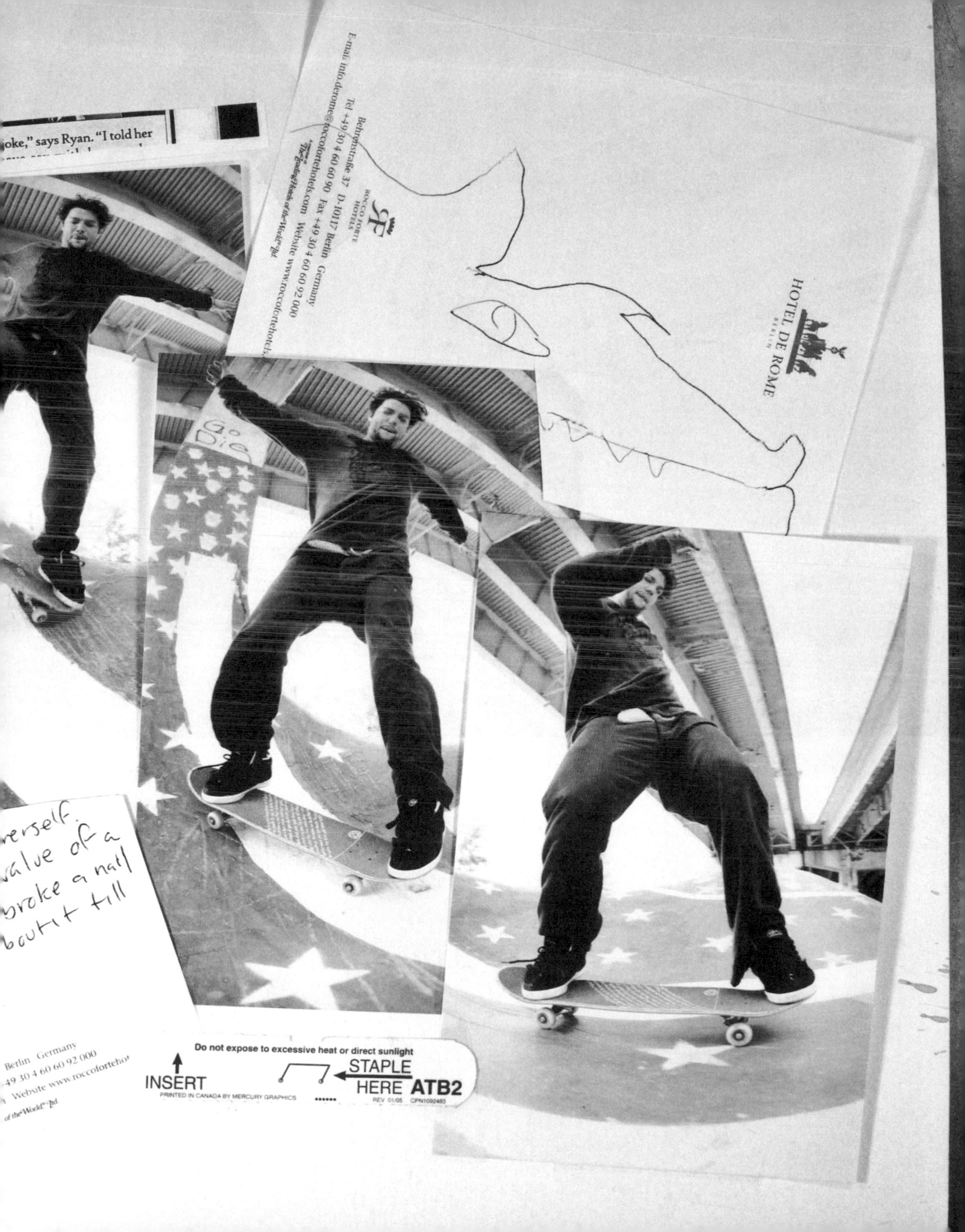

joke," says Ryan. "I told her

Go
Die

rself.
value of a
broke a nail
bout it till

$1,700 →

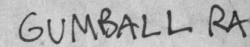
GUMBALL RA

No: 25 153 Dups: 02.
DOB: 09/28/1979 Sex: M
Class: C Eyes: BL
Endorse: Height: 5'06"
Com/Med Rstr: */*
Issued: 12/03/2001
Expires: 09/30/2003

BRANDON C MARGERA
2 GRAYHAWK LN
THORNTON PA 19373

DL

$250,000 →

# Chateau Marmont
## hollywood

April 2006

Just got pulled over going 167 miles
per fucking hour on the 10 freeway in
Los Angeles with ryan Dunn. The cop
gave me 5 citations - speeding

   - wreckless
     endangerment
   - no seatbelts

   - passing people
     on the shoulder
     of an inorsecfon

   - beer in the
     car

I lost my liscence for 2 months
but im still driving.

8221 SUNSET BOULEVARD   HOLLYWOOD CALIFORNIA 90046

TELEPHONE (323) 656-1010  FACSIMILE (323) 655-5311

| | | | all day |
|---|---|---|---|
| 2  3  4  5  6  7  8<br>9  10  11  12  13  14  15<br>16  17  18  19  20  21  22<br>23  24  25  26  27  28  29<br>30  31 | | | Restaurant festival<br>IRON HILL<br>3 KILDARES |
| **5**<br>Skated<br>Driveway<br>200 sit ups<br><br>CKY @ READING<br>Hopped on tourbus<br>w/ MISSY<br>*Labor Day* | **6**<br>chilled w/ cky<br>in NY<br>Bought Fraggle rock<br><br>Sound check<br>CKY IN NY!<br>stayed at Carson<br>Daly's house | **7**<br>4:56 meeting<br>MTV meeting in<br>NY<br>Drove to west chester<br>watched Rongren for<br>a dream<br>Jenn breaks into the<br>fucking house at 4am<br>COPS came | **8**<br>Private Jet<br>to<br>San Diego<br><br>ASR TRADES HOW |
| **12**<br>drove home from<br>Ocean city NJ<br>Got Laptop @ applestore<br>300 sit ups<br><br>FIREWATERS, DUFFERS!<br>69 and Fucked | **13**<br>Fly to<br><br>FT. WAYNE<br>INDIANA,<br><br>DINNER w/ John Cougar<br>mellencamp | **14**<br>450 SIT UPS<br><br>Demo<br>FT. WAYNE<br>INDIANA | **15**<br>300 SITUPS<br><br>Fly to<br>CAYMAN<br>ISLAND<br><br>Skated the<br>BLACK PEARL |
| **19**<br>Flew home from<br>ATLANTA<br>400 sit ups<br>Kerry came over<br>Skated delaware w/ Nate<br>RADIO BAM!<br>xcona w/ Missy, Rog, Nate<br>BOWLING IN DOWNINGTOWN<br>HUGO POOL | **20**<br>Season 5<br>Commentary for VL8<br>IN PHILADELPHIA<br><br>Meeting w/ saturn<br>@ kildares<br><br>Went to Blarney st.<br>+ kildares | **21**<br>peppermill w/ missy<br>Got Message in wc<br>went to Birds+bees<br>Fucked<br>Read novak book<br><br>went to Jess's | **22**<br>Edit HIM documenta<br>for MTV2<br>Got fitted for TUX<br>300 sit ups<br>Looked @ greystone<br>mansion for CKY vide<br>Goose cook<br>300 more sit ups<br>kildares   150 more<br>Gregs house   Radio<br><br>*Autumnal Equinox<br>6:23 P* |
| **26**<br><br>LA | **27**<br><br><br>did shopping cart | **28** | **29**<br>Brandon Dicos<br>house<br>sushi |

How many more ways

# BamMargera

'Pacific blue'
ent to brans
dited Him documentary
A meeting
north w/ Antny bloodhun
ex's saw thieves

Gill
Kerry airs
King of prussa
Bought huge n
Saw 40 yr ol
300 more si

9

San Diego

Skated the
driveway w/R
Hoof, Nate br
skated eas

Conecall C
Giveawa

skate eas

watch Cine

0 SITUPS

16

500 SITU

ONTREAL
UEBEC

189

IM in Colorado filming a VLB episode called "Groundhog day" and I cant drinks for 10 days cause im preparing To do the LOOP in Pheonce, AZ for the tony Hawk boom boom huck Jam. We Are at copper MT. and Novak is passed out in the snow after dancing with his pants off standing on the bar. This will be my 3rd time trying the Loop. I ate shit in florida for jackass, then tried it at bob burnquests and nearly did it but my legs were giving out on the 20th attempt so I had to stop. Now in 10 days im ginng it another GO!

ARIZON
Just land
the LooP
1st try afte
tAking the pa
away!!! 13th
Person to ever
it! wahoo! This M
Mexican news reporte
wanted to fuck me the
night but I got too
drunk and blew it.
Passed out in my roo
and woke up to a stra
overweight girl on my
dick saying "I love you
I love you! I love you!"
I flipped her off of me an
screamed. She was the mo
regretful Hump ive ever
Fucked hands Down!

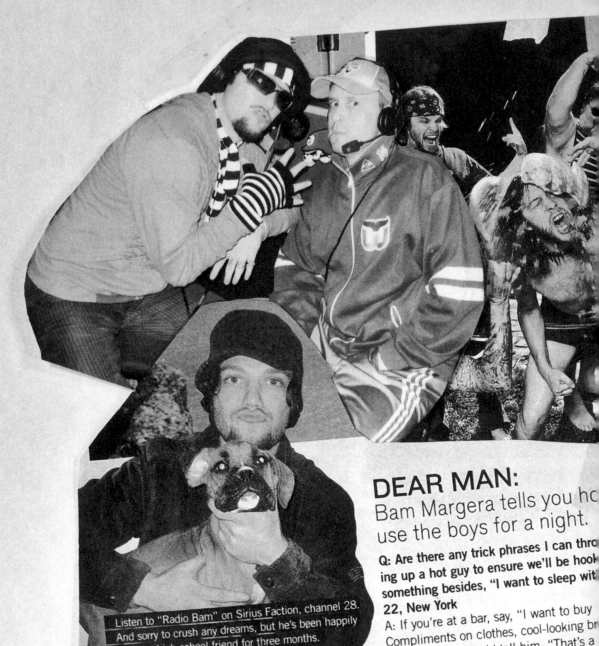

Listen to "Radio Bam" on Sirius Faction, channel 28. And sorry to crush any dreams, but he's been happily dating a high school friend for three months.

## DEAR MAN:
Bam Margera tells you ho[w to] use the boys for a night.

**Q: Are there any trick phrases I can thro[w]** ing up a hot guy to ensure we'll be hook[ed] something besides, "I want to sleep wit[h] 22, New York

A: If you're at a bar, say, "I want to buy [you] Compliments on clothes, cool-looking br[...] also good. You could tell him, "That's a [...] does it mean?" That always works—I get stringed into tattoos since I'm still totally stoked on all of them. I co[uld] music for eight hours straight. But, yeah—don't say, "[...]" Sometimes I run into sketchy rock chicks and they'll b[...] forward, like, "I wanna take you to my room." It would[...] chosen different words. They make it way too easy—th[...] You'd go up to their room, and you probably couldn't w[...] [t]he worst—this girl walks up to me at a bar and slaps [...] [d]umped it on her head. Turns out she was a fan of [...] [w]ould enjoy it if a stranger smacked me in [...]

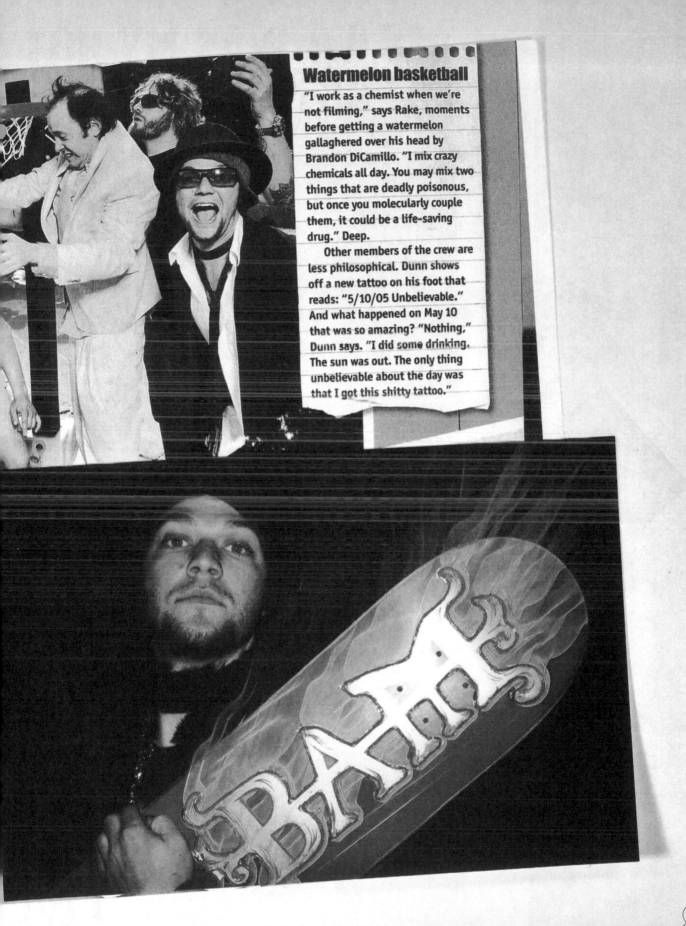

## Watermelon basketball

"I work as a chemist when we're not filming," says Rake, moments before getting a watermelon gallaghered over his head by Brandon DiCamillo. "I mix crazy chemicals all day. You may mix two things that are deadly poisonous, but once you molecularly couple them, it could be a life-saving drug." Deep.

Other members of the crew are less philosophical. Dunn shows off a new tattoo on his foot that reads: "5/10/05 Unbelievable." And what happened on May 10 that was so amazing? "Nothing," Dunn says. "I did some drinking. The sun was out. The only thing unbelievable about the day was that I got this shitty tattoo."

At the time of these Rake Yohn photo I woul
the perfect heavy metal poster child. Thats why
on the cover of CKY2k! Now Rake is a chomost
him tuck his shirts into his Khki pants   Ahaha!

BY APRIL 1ST APRIL F

**NOW I HAVE MY OWN**
**WHATEVER I WA**
**I WA**

POT UNTIL JERKOFFS
AND WOULDN'T LET ME
BREAK A SWEAT!!

BAM

ARK AND I CAN DO
AND INVITE WHOEVER
AAAHHAHAHAHAHAHA!!!!!!!

V

"yo dudes i got kicked out of school today!"

"your dad is gonna kill you"

CUT TO

"Get in the carding bat"

"Back in the war we killed cissys like u"

---

"Cease and desist, u cant work on ur invention?"

CUT TO

"Sweet circonia Beast"

CUT TO

SHOOTING

"This means war!"

CUT TO

(CAR BARRELS THROUGH GARAGE)

CUT TO

"Dominick the filty crookes one breaking into the werehouse"

Cut to

"that money is born to be mine!"

(knife Hitting rut ru's face)

---

LENNY GOLF CART KICK →

★ CEASE AND DESIST, U CANT WORK ON YO INVENTION?

★ THIS MEANS WAR

★ PONCE ON FIRE

★ THIS IS MY KIND OF MOVIE

★ AMBULANCE HIT

★ DOM WICK WHAT ARE YOU MAKING US WATCH?

THINGS TO THROW IN IF NEEDED

A.) SCOTTY LEDUCHE SPINNING AND LAUGHING

B.) LENNY HITTING MACROGANS WALL

C.) TUCKER DESTROYING DINNER PLATES

D.) "THAT MONEY WAS BORN TO BE MINE"
(SHOW RUT RU WITH THE MONEY)

E.) "I HEAR YA'S TALKIN ABOUT ME IN THERE!"

F.) DUDESONS FALLING OUT OF TREE

6.) VITO DEVIL "RUT RU SOX"

H.) "TUCKER WERE CHEERING FOR YOU"

I.) Both needles in the ass.

---

Libby → "Meet me upstairs in one of the bedrooms"

CUT TO

TUCKER AND BAGGER IN BED

Libby → "What the hell is going on here?"

Ralph → "I thought i found true love!"

CUT TO

Phil → "hey bruno, its the gay gazette and hes on the cover!"

CUT TO

Don vito → "My nephews gay!"

---

Lenny → "YOU DO KNOW THERE IS A KNIF FIGHT AT THE TRAILER PARK"
(SHOW HAIN WITH THE SHOVEL)

Tucker → "I KNOW IM GONNA TALK LIBBY INTO LIKING ME AGAIN"

CUT TO

Tucker → "I MADE THIS FOR YOU"

Libby → "IT SUCKS"

CUT TO

BRUNO KARATE CHOP

When a rich jerk seduces your mom and steals your cool invention, it's time to get even!

BAM MARGERA PRESENTS

MiNGHAGS THE MOVIE! ®

Bam Margera          Brandon DiCamillo          Ryan Dunn          Rake Yohn
Mark The Bagger      Don Vito      Phillip Margera Sr.      Brandon Novak
Ruthie "Boof" Margera      April Margera      Phil Margera      Gina Lynn
David "Lord" Bottaro   Angie Cuturic   Ted Trullinger   Missy Margera
"Compton Ass" Terry Kennedy   The Bloodhound Gang   The Dudesons
Writers / Executive Producers   Bam Margera   Joe Frantz   Brandon DiCamillo
Production Designer Seth Meisterman   Director Of Photography Joe Frantz

6.4.0

We have 3 more days of minghags filming
left and i have been shitbag washed basically the entire shoot and forgot missys birthday.
She talked me into going to rehab in arizona,
the same shit kate moss went to, now im on
the airplane reconsidering this shit, i have
a layover in denver and slomb is meeting me
For the one hour i have to get the next flight
to tuscon, i dont think rehab is for me, i
will simply just not drink, i will find out
my final desicion in 30 minutes when
this flight lands. By the way i am writing
this is cause the fuckass next to me wont
stop talking And asking me dumb questions.
So much for first class!

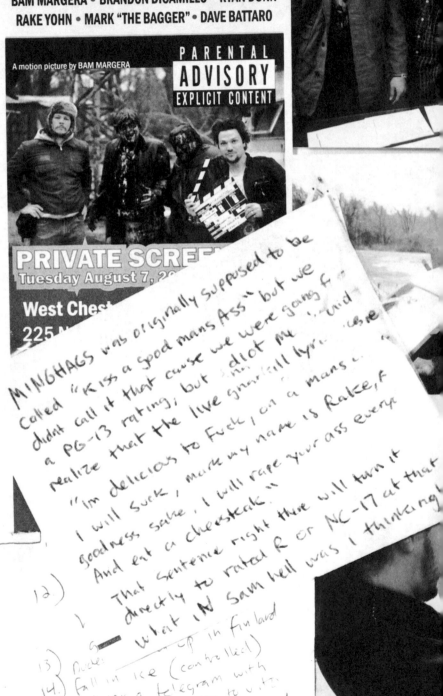

MINGHAGS

BAM MARGERA • BRANDON DICAMILLO • RYAN DUNN
RAKE YOHN • MARK "THE BAGGER" • DAVE BATTARO

A motion picture by BAM MARGERA

PARENTAL
ADVISORY
EXPLICIT CONTENT

PRIVATE SCREE...
Tuesday August 7, 2...

West Chest...
225 N...

MINGHAGS was originally supposed to be called "Kiss a good mans Ass" but we didn't call it that cause we were going for a PG-13 rating; but ...diot me ...and realize that the live gnarkill lyrics...re "im delicios to Fuck, on a mans ... I will suck, mark my name is Rake, f goodness sake, I will rape your ass every And eat a cheesteak"...

12)

That sentence right there will turn it directly to rated R or NC-17 at that what in sam hell was i thinking!

13) ...up in Finland
14) fall in ice (controlled)
15) deliver a telegram with remote helecopter to ...this is a bad

ress, golf
n down, edit,
s, golf to calm
wn, Edit, stress
olf to calm down.

Tattersall reprezent!

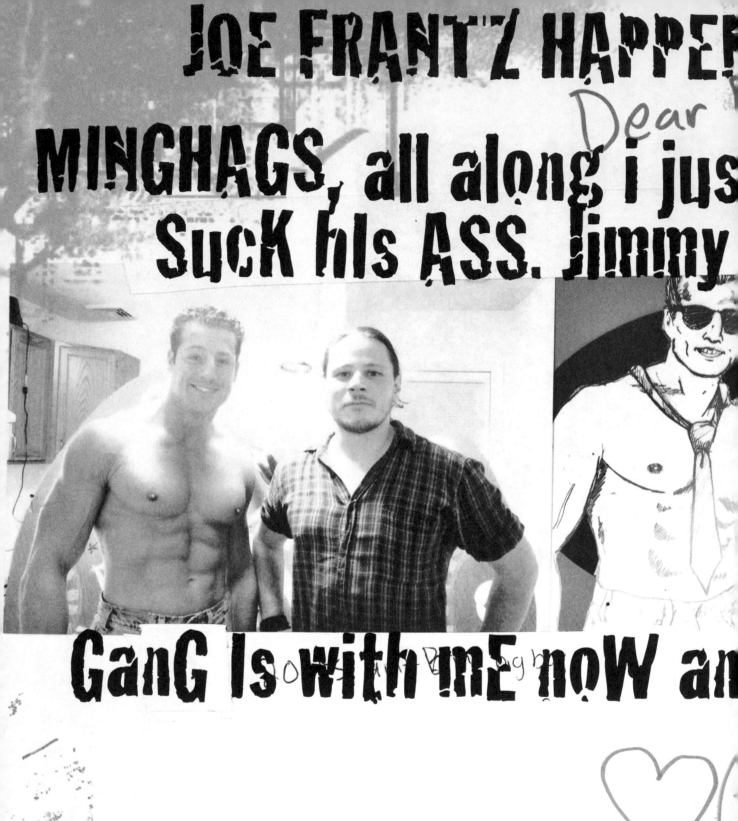

D TO FIND "BRUNO" FOR

am
think Frantz wanted to
OP frOm The BlooDhOUNd

OU'RE THE
BEST...
AND YOU
STILL ARE!

he totally aGreeS ....

Bruno!

StILL ArE - BRUNO

PROJECT _____ DATE _____

Thanks to a 20 hour flight
from Australia and Valium,
Managed to rip my hamstring,
ass and groin on a smith grind
down 13 stairs. Note to self:
Dont skate after long plane
rides!

"what would you say if every time you took out the trash you could have delicious juice!"

would you?
would you like it?
i drew mine.

if it's yours then it wa
be more like

discussing

Better.

OTING MINGHAGS

How can your stomach be Rumbling when you eat this much!?

AT TATTERSALL

① April 20-22 Louisville, KY 83

② may 18-20 Grand Praire, TX   X-trials

③ june 15-17 Bristol, CT   X-trials

④ june 22-24 copenhagen, DE
        30-1   germany
    July 6-8   biaritz
        13-15   prauge

Aug 17-23 philly X-games

HM BOX

3 barn boards

HOMO'S W/ MUL

# MINGHABS

you are guilty

you owe the yuppie family one
million dollars for disrupting their
precious morning

you owe 8 million dollars for
getting chocolate sauce all over
the gays GUILTY

you owe 5 million dollars to
Libby parents for the stupid thing
turning into a vicious robot

Court adjourned

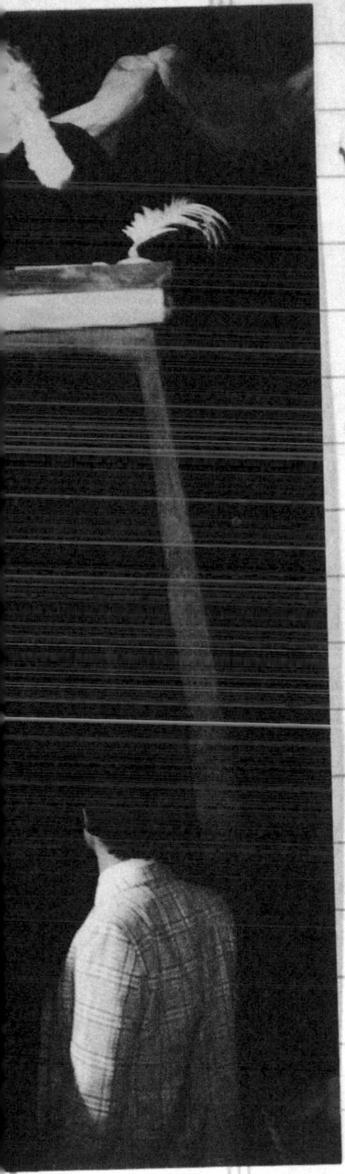

Beware of
Killer K

**7. FILTERING:** After proper conditioning, the beer is sent through a filter [G] to remove all traces of the yeast before it is transferred to the serving tanks [H].

**8. SERVING:** Finally, the beer carbonation level is adjusted and it is ready to be sent to our taps for consumption. From start to finish our beers travel less than 65 feet. There's nothing fresher!

# MINGHAGS

Get in the car Dingbat!

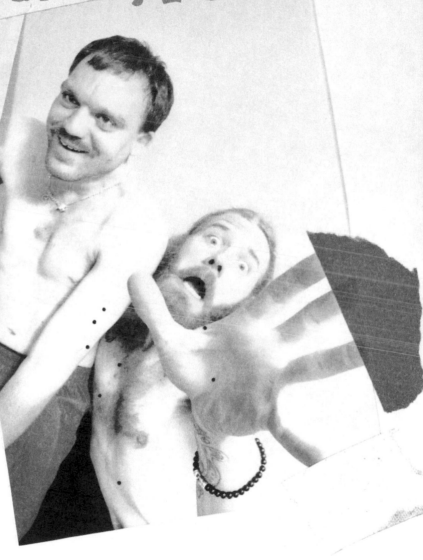

pissed all over

Octobre ✤ October
10•2006

LUN • MON

7am Golf time
w/ Gene @
Valley National

MAR • TU

Washed the ...

2

KOP

Belvédère Huron, parc de la Gatineau
Sugar Maples at Huron Lookout, Gatineau Park

SAM · SAT

7

VEN · FRI

Mont-Marts Waterfall

6

Le Quebec
to
PHILADELPHIE

ZORRO ON DOUGHNUTS

JEU · THURS

5

went shoppin and
shit with missy in
Quebec

MER · WED

4

Rode the fuckin 4wheeler
to the airport cause all
the cars were gone

3

Flew to
Quebec
CITY
stayed @
Le Château
Frontenac

...eet @
...attersall
...scription Addal
...usage by carla
...GN 57 CAFE
Syracuse Taussy

element

ele...

octor has to sew on a ripped of dick
earn extra for a handling fee? Some
hink about!

**SHOOT** 2007

**Amy Harris**
Phone 3666 6016
Email harrisa@qnp.newsltd.com.au

**Phil Bartsch**
Phone 5584 2870
Email bartschp@qnp.newsltd.com.au

TED A STAR? GIVE US A CALL

*Handwritten note:*

10·17·07

I took missy to Australia for 8 days thinking we would have some nice vacation time, instead it was me hosting 8 one hour countdown episodes for MTV, 7 phone interviews and 5 autograph signings down the east coast that were 3 blocks down the street. Each day was 4 to 5 hrs of signing. I don't even got to SK8. Luckly I bumped into Linkin Park the last day and I actually got to take missy to a concert and escape!

# Bam the man for local fans

SKATE king and MTV *Jackass* member **Bam Margera** made it to Brisbane yesterday for an in-store promotion although he acted, and was revered by the teenagers, more like a rock star than a balancing freak.

Bam, who had only stepped off the plane a couple of hours beforehand, walked into City Beach in the Queen St Mall with a drink, of the top-shelf variety, mind you, in his hand and a broad smile on his face.

The queue of teens lined up to see the cable TV personality snaked through the store and at least 100m through the mall.

Extra security had to be rounded up to handle the gathering and also to answer the store's shoplifting alarms which rang like a government complaints hotline.

By Bam's side was his wife of eight months **Missy**, whom he met when they were in seventh grade and was part of their reality MTV show.

"This is pretty amazing," said Missy as she panned the store.

"I've had about 30 or 40 jobs in my life from waitressing to being a nanny, but now I mainly assist Bam."

In budapest, i met C.O.B.
Singer Alexi @ Lobby bar and
we polish off an entire bottle
of Tillamore dew. I bet him I will
jump off the budapest bridge by
the end of the day for $200.
The next morning i see him and
He says "you owe me $200"
i say bullshit fagit i already
did it. Here's Living
Proof!!

"His foot seems to be a magnet for pain recently," I said. "He just broke his foot in three places riding motorcycles."

"Oh, that sucks," Knoxville said. "He'll be so bummed because he can't skate."

"But the Hummer?" I said. I fucking hate [Hummer]s, I had to know how to destroy them. "What [did you] do to it? Did you take a chainsaw to it?"

"No, it was a Saw Gall? A Sawl? Saws All thing?" [he sai]d finally. "And you can saw through those sons [of bitc]hes pretty easy, you know? Just get a Saws All [and go] to a parking lot and have a ball."

see me.

Oh, that does sound fun.

But yet another thing I wish all those Bam fans would emulate is their hero's favorite pastime: skateboarding. It's way more fun than a "heartagram" tattoo. What the hell is a heartagram, anyway? I have to admit I kind of like the way it looks, but what does that mean, "sensitive evil?" That makes about as much sense as "compassionate conservatism."

"Do you even skate anymore?" I asked him.

"If I have twenty minutes filming break," he said, "I'll go skate the mini ramp with like Tim Glom, sometimes Tim O'Connor and Kerry Getz

are here. If I have a full day off I'[ll go] and skate. That's the thing, I do[n't like] going into Philadelphia and sk[ate] and getting kicked out. Fuck, I [go to] the Philly park and skate all d[ay and get] kicked out. It's way more fun [to skate] unless I have like a month to [travel to] go to like Australia or whateve[r and get] city spots. I have all this footag[e coming] out right now. I'm really psyche[d. Bam] likes it so much they want to s[how it] or something."

S 118

Were on the South island of New Zealand and I see this 50 ft bridge with a massive current lead. Out to the sea, I didnt know how deep it was, but I didnt care. when the fuck is the next time I will be here? I asked my self. Fuck it I jumped and slammed to the bottom, 6ft deep! ow.

O°13

Pivotal moment. Brandon Novak, Oxford

I came up with a skit called the human raccoon, which basically consists of punching your buddies eyes out till they are completely black and blue. Then put him in a raccoon outfit and paint his face. We did this with novak for jackass 2 but it never made it. All we got out of the deal was a cool radio show!

# AT STATE OF BAM, THE SPINE RAMP WAS THIS SKATING IN AVONDALE, PA

I'm on the tony hawk gigantic skatepark tour and we arrive to louisville kentucky at midnight, I know we have a demo infront of 5,000 kids the next day at a huge cement skatepark that I have never skated. So I want to cruise the park at night to get a feel for what were getting ourselves into tomorrow. Sure enough I head right for the 20ft tall full pipe and head toward it at full speed. Just at about 13 ft is where the over vert is and im headed right at it as my front foot slips of the board in mid air. I fly head first from 13ft above knocking myself out unconcious. The whole team rushes down to carry me out of the gigantic bowl and rushing me to the hospital. I was cat scanned with a concosion and a ripped liver and they were not letting me leave until they knew it was healing. 3 days I was in that fucking hospital and I had to take a private jet home for $10,000 because I couldnt walk through the airport. definitely top 3 out of my worst slams!

**INJURIES!**

I'm driving home from 50 cents house and evil jared from the bloodhound gang calls and says there filming cribs and for me to drive the banana car into the mote. The mote was a 6ft drop and jared said its 7ft deep. So I drive full speed into the mote thinking im gonna get fucked up, sure enough no injuries, so then like an idiot I do a gainer off the top of the car and under rotate causing me to go in head first. The fucking mote was only 2 feet deep! I cracked my head open causing 15 staples in my fucking head!

Flew into kentucky for an adio demo at a
massive concrete park at midnight and I wanted
to get a feel for the park before the big demo
the next day. its pitch black out and I go right
towards the 20ft full pipe and go way over vert
causing me to fall from 13ft above right to
my fucking head knocking myself out and a ripped
liver from the fucking ribs. went to the hospital for
3 days and had a private jet take me home for $10,000
because I could walk through the airport.

The chronicles of GNAR KILL!

# DAVOS, SWIT

2003

B
A

ERLAND

H. IT'S ALL NEW BlooD 2:59
S. UGLINESS SH*T 4:57
V.I.P. 5:56
6:58

ds America. Inc.. 338 N. Foothill Roa
ecords America. Inc. All rights reserved. Warning: Unauth-
'pop
m

CONTROLLED
PLACEBO

Beer + Ice = Ic

This is the day Before Ville w
Rehab in LA, he stayed up a
any thing he could Find. Voc
wine, pills, etc The next mor
meeting with warriers at che
and he was drinking warm
had an asthma attack. I wa
i told him i was calling an a
an hour, he Freaked out an

Promises
t drinkins
whisked, Red
e had a
sharmont
roger and
scared
nce. after
for rehab.

B+B,
good tidings I bring, to you and your Sir
All the best in love + health —
Nice to know you
x Melissa x

old beer!

Stevie and I say "Happy New
and see ya

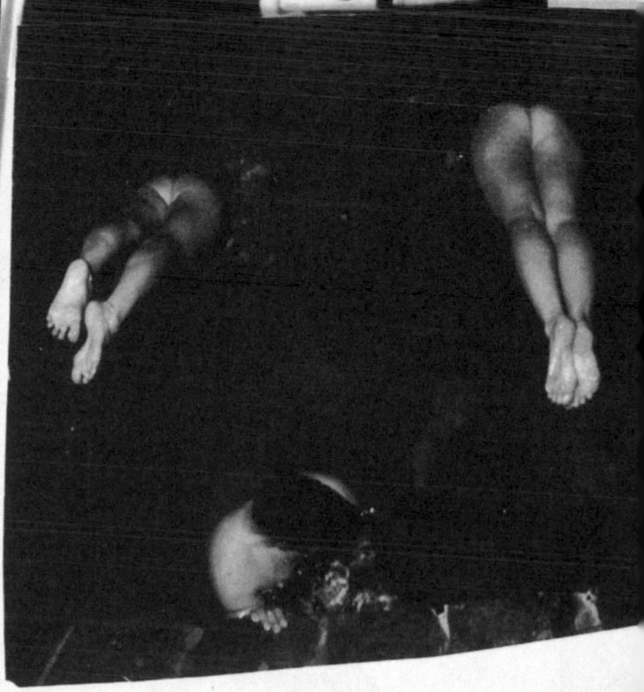

BURNT FLOOR

1:15AM
FISH FRY TURNS INTO GLOMB FRY
ND DEGREE BURN ON THE NECK

So glomb and I
Camping trip to
Rushmore then hea
Horse, Lake house on
caught 3 fish, I b
Prepares a fishfry
alone in a 2 million
oil on the pan catc
Glomb drops the p
curtains up in flam
Panicked and opened
throw the pan out
wind blew move
was a $10,000 mista
Parents. And the
it all is that I w
DRUNK for on

OKABOJI

...ted to take a skate/
...lackhills to see mt...
...his girlfriends parents...
...n at lake okaboji. we...
...u and a perch. Glomb...
...e way we are completely...
...lake house) and the...
...re, a big fire! And...
...ghting the couch and...
...ong with his face, I...
...liding glass door to...
...a massive gust...
...on more shit. It...
...d pissed off some...
...est thing about...
...even fuck...

TED + KATHY Stuart,
thank for letting us stay.
Sorry I almost burned it
down. Not a good first time stay...
The men here are nice though.
Steaks in fridge were a...
pre-fire "thankyou". I'm sure
the floor + couch will require a
bigger "sorry" gift.
Tim & Brian

BAM

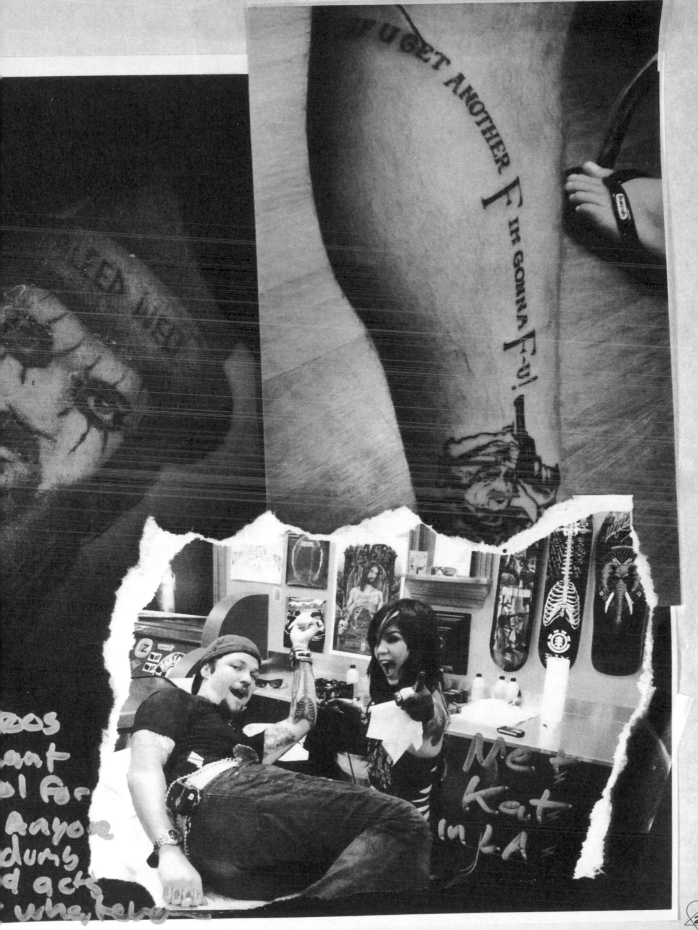

I know what I want out of life, before I had too many things. Too many things that weren't mine and nothing mattered if something was broke, ~~and~~ it would just get replaced. I dont want a house decorated the way my mom wants it, I want to do it on my own. If you dont do normal things like laundry, dishes, organizing your things then you will pre occupy that time with something unproductive. Everything in this tiny room in Barcelona is mine, I picked them out myself. The people in this house are hungry, motivated skaters who NEED to do the next best trick to survive. I dont need fancy restaurants and I dont need to be at a bar everynight. I need that time to think and skate the next day. I dont need medicine from the doctor to make me feel better. skateboarding is my medicine? I need to use my legs as much as possible. Living in a city makes you do that and you will always experience something new and interesting even if you are walking the same route. I NEED TO START FROM SCRATCH AND REMEMBER WHAT ITS LIKE TO HAVE NOTHING!

# Day 2 (where the fuck is santa?)

We all have flights out of JFK at 8pm, I realize once again my fuckin passport is M.I.A., i rip my room apart digging through all my clothes for 2 fuckin hours and nothing. Now its 6am and I have to get into the production Van to the passport agency in Philly for a $400 rush job. After 3 hours of bullshit I know have a new passport and get picked up in the hummer with The posse (C16, Jess, Fanna, Novak, Frantz) off to JFK whea Fanna is shittossed from Jameson and hes attempting to hit on a girl, but his slurring words and knocking over some drinks got him nowhere! Off to Finland!

LAYOVER AT LONDON HEATHROW 4 DAYS BEFOR

ay 'S Hellzinki

e arrive to Vaanta airport in
lzinki at 10 am and the schedule
tight. The whole point of the trip
to make it 600 miles north to
e arctic circle so theres no
me for sleep. Not to mention
ere are a lot of rocker friends
mine to see. so first stop,
osturi, HIM's rehearsal studio
o I can ask them for some
iking adivce to santas and
o hear some live new rockin
shit'. Ville draws a map on
annas belly to show us the
vay but his sweaty belly was
washing off the marker and
e werent about to be lost
n the middle of the arctic
woods in the freezing cold, so ville called his tattoo buddy
y Juho to meet us at the top of tornii which is the tallest
building in Helsinki for fanna to have a nice view
while we gave him the shittiest tattoo on earth.' way
to go!

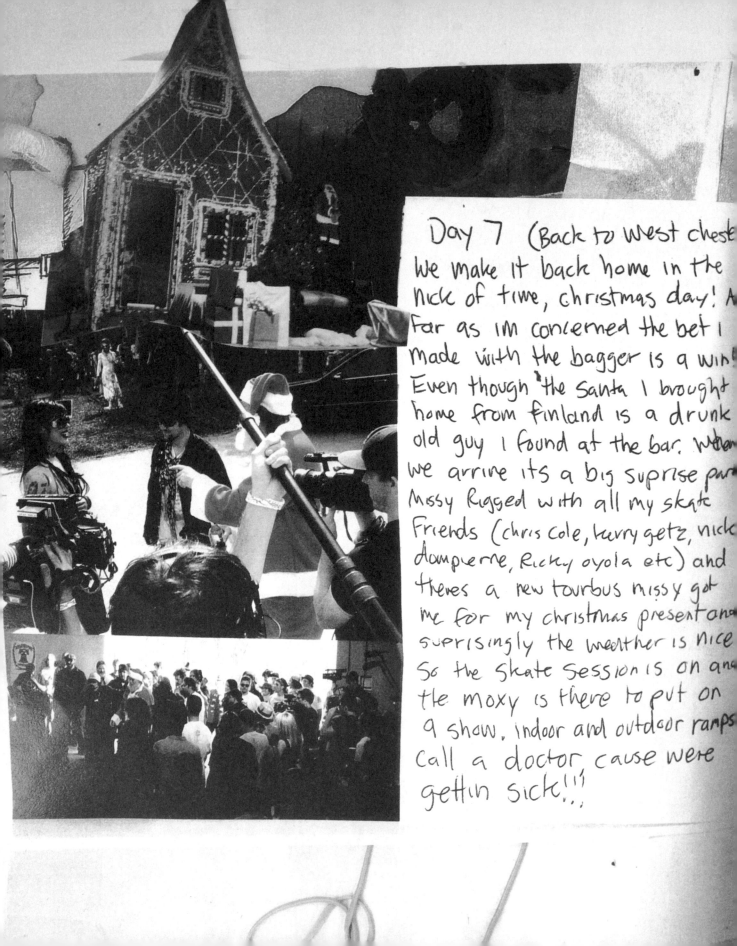

Day 7 (Back to West chest
We make it back home in the
nick of time, christmas day! A
far as im concerned the bet i
made with the bagger is a win
Even though the santa I brought
home from finland is a drunk
old guy i found at the bar. When
we arrive its a big suprise par
Missy Rigged with all my skate
friends (chris cole, kerry getz, nick
dompierre, Ricky oyola etc) and
theres a new tourbus missy got
me for my christmas present and
suprisingly the weather is nice
so the skate session is on and
the moxy is there to put on
a show. indoor and outdoor ramps
call a doctor cause were
gettin sick!!!

It was Midnight and I was Leaving winkles house AkA the
Parallel skatehouse. I had 2 big bags filled with shit I bought
for Missy and a pair of all black half cabs. The First pair of
skateshoes I bought in 10 years and I was so stoked to skate in
them for the next week of filming with Kerry Getz in Barcelona. It
was the first time I had to walk alone at night, it was a
2 mile walk through some alleys and then up a windy Hill to
fancy hotel mirimar. As soon as im out the door I make eye
contact with some shady fuck walking in the opposite direct
think to myself why do I think this guy is going to follow
turn around to tal

A quick peek and what do you know, he's now following me and there's not a person in sight. The worst part is I know I have to make a left onto a darker alley for 3 blocks into a shadier part of town. I start walking faster and so does the cocksucker who wants my bags. Now I start running and he does as well. I finally make it to the massive steep hill that is about a mile up and my legs are giving up from all the skating we've been doing all day. I stop to think as this dude is coming closer and closer. Fuck it! I just started running, I sprinted up this steep ass hill until he finally gave up. I made it to the ned Hotel with jello legs but I still have my New skate shoes!

Note to self- dont walk alone at Night with a city your not familiar with. Especially when your carrying shit you really like !!!

P.S. if your in Barcelona, go to the Bottom of monjuic mountain and try sprinting up that shit with 2 heavy bags. It's a pain in the ass, it sucks and youll hate it!!

Jackass week Radio faction

Finish it in Spain and s to ch A so

superstar- wake up dead
- theatweaker
- Life burns
y you lived
ydown

a damn

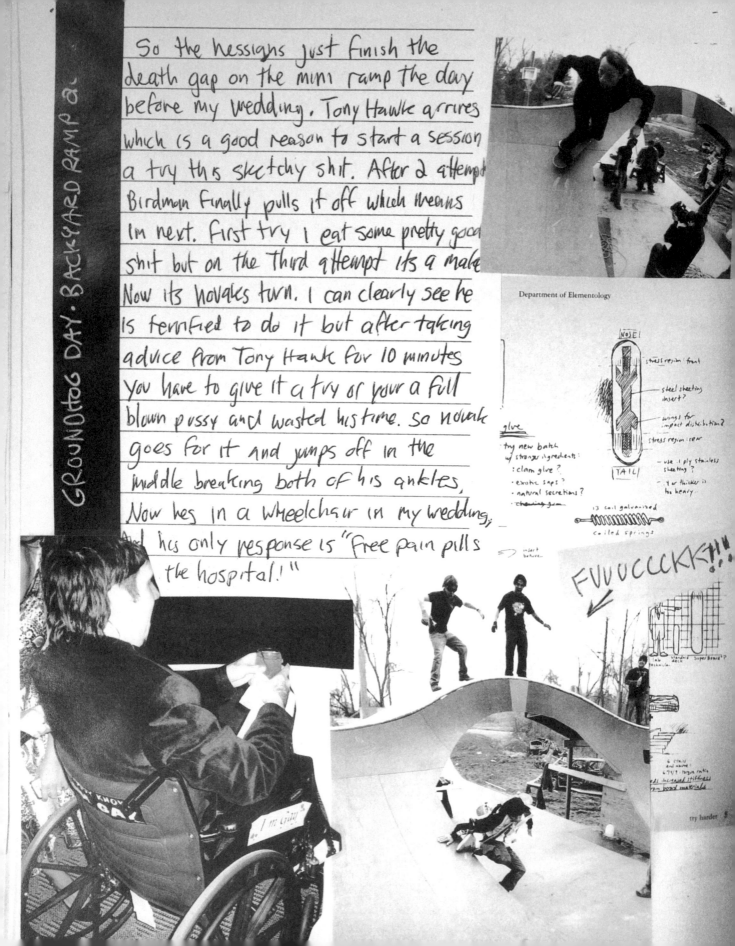

So the hessigns just finish the death gap on the mini ramp the day before my wedding. Tony Hawk arrives which is a good reason to start a session a try this sketchy shit. After 2 attempts Birdman finally pulls it off which means I'm next. First try I eat some pretty good shit but on the third attempt its a make. Now its novaks turn. I can clearly see he is terrified to do it but after taking advice from Tony Hawk for 10 minutes you have to give it a try or your a full blown pussy and wasted his time. So novak goes for it and jumps off in the middle breaking both of his ankles, Now hes in a wheelchair in my wedding, And his only response is "free pain pills the hospital!"

Department of Elementology

NOSE!

stress region front

steel sheeting insert?

wings for impact distribution?

stress region rear

use 1 ply stainless sheeting?

4 or thicker is too heavy.

TAIL!

glve

try new batch of stronger ingredients:

: clam glue ?

· exotic saps ?

· natural secretions ?

· chewing gum

13 coil galvanised

coiled springs

insert before.

FUUUCCCKKK!!!

standard SuperBoard?

lab technician

deck

6 colors and above? 6.7/1 torque ratio eds increased stiffness from board materials

try harder

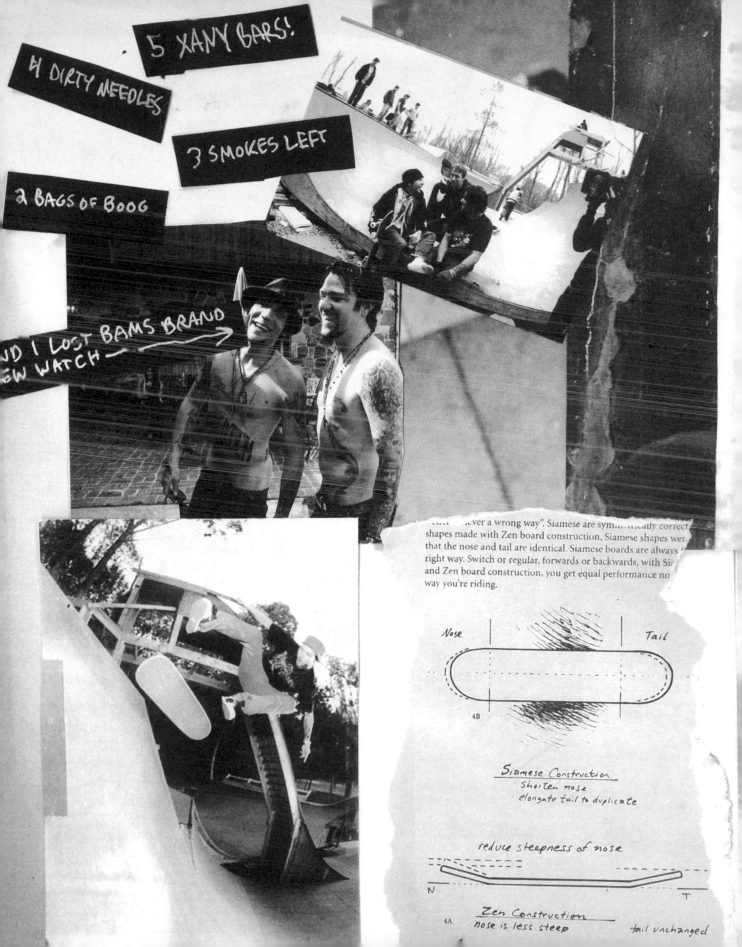

5 XANY BARS!

4 DIRTY NEEDLES

3 SMOKES LEFT

2 BAGS OF BOOG

ND I LOST BAMS BRAND EW WATCH →

...ever a wrong way". Siamese are symmetrically correct shapes made with Zen board construction, Siamese shapes wer... that the nose and tail are identical. Siamese boards are always... right way. Switch or regular, forwards or backwards, with Si... and Zen board construction, you get equal performance no... way you're riding.

Nose                    Tail

4B

Siamese Construction
  Shorten nose
  elongate tail to duplicate

reduce steepness of nose

N                       T

Zen Construction
4A    nose is less steep              tail unchanged

Lou
Goyle!

My Name's Louie
I'm in the Moxy
And one day
I will play at
the Roxy!
My name's Louie,
I wear chinese
sneakers!

Im in new hope at chads
_ing to New cky songs live!
_the next day (we stayed over)
_ has a 104 fever and _
_els practice, now, we have
_other option than to drink
_er and iced teas at
_ and peters. Lawrence,
_ Lou gayle decides to
_ every drink that I get.
_keep in mind hes 23,
_ 24, so i know the drill.
_inds up barfing in the
_es and then passes out!
_ railroad tracks in the
_es, Like ray brower,
_ of sort of, this is
_vn on sentence, anyway
_e he is, as ray brower

# TAND BY ME! ↗

Its 11am on a hot summer day and I come down from my room looking a 6 dudes crashed on the couches and floor. Must have been from the rager last night, well why not continue the mission. As I crack. open a pbr tallboy and people start to wake up I get the bright idea to go to the junk yard to buy 8 cars for $8,000 as glomb builds me a launch ramp over the garage, yes thats right! we are going to put bricks on the gas pedals of cars and launch them over the garage! hours later we comeback with a shitload of cars and were ready to rock. I forgot to mention I had just broke up with my now x-girlfriend and all of her stuff is in bags in the garage who would have thought that the very first car we try misses the entire ramp and plows through the garage Sideways knocking every last paint can into the x's shit. she shows up the next day looking at the damage calling me everyo name in the book. i tried to tell her we were simply trying to launch cars over the garage and she simply wasnt buying it. But fuckin hell it was the actual truth. By the way the 5th car jump was golden!!!

I decided to fishtail the limo into the pool and it worked beautifully. But I was not satisfied, so I started up shitbirds jeep and drove that in as well. Bad Move. I owed him $2000! that piece of shit aint worth that!

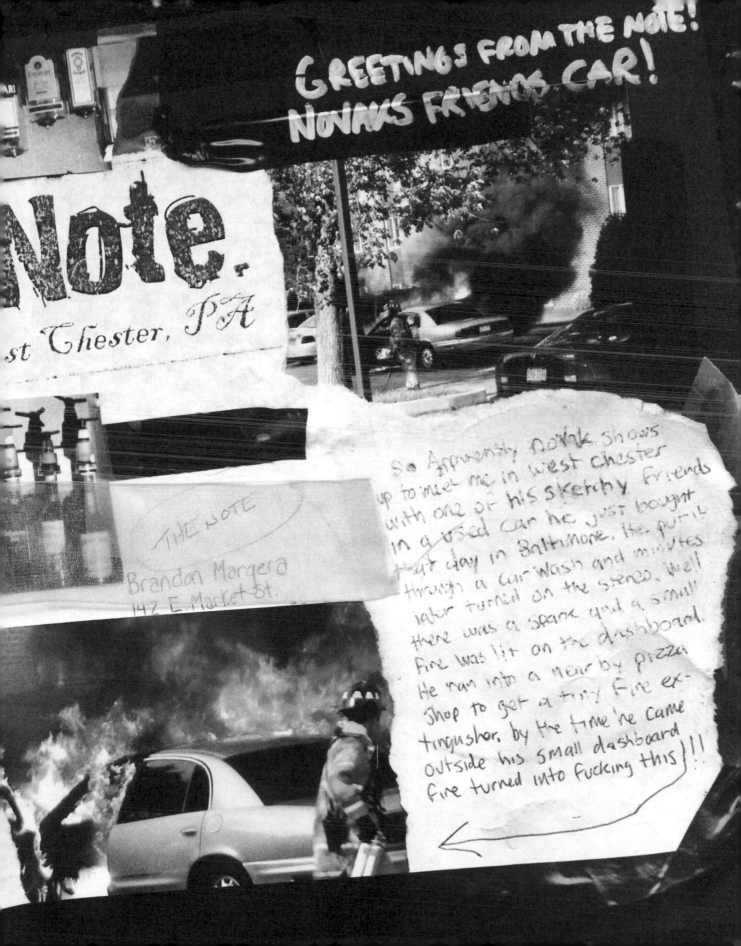

GREETINGS FROM THE NOTE!
NOVAKS FRIENDS CAR!

Note.
st Chester, PA

THE NOTE
Brandon Margera
142 E. Market St.

So Apparently Novak shows up to meet me in west chester with one of his sketchy friends in a used car he just bought that day in Baltimore. He pull through a car wash and minutes later turned on the stereo. Well there was a spark and a small fire was lit on the dashboard. He ran into a nearby pizza shop to get a tiny fire extingushor. by the time he came outside his small dashboard fire turned into fucking this!!!

CAMDEN TOWN 3:45 am — this dipshit moron idiot comes to london with $50 dollars in his pocket and spends it all on 8 boxes of Kentucky fried chicken for 3 people. What a shithead! The other 5 boxes we left there. I hope a few bums ate it! Fuckin idiot!

NOVAKS NEW VITAMIN: CABERNET SAUVIGNON
TIERRA ANTICA CHILE 2007

CAMDEN TOWN

SHOPPING (LIKE ZOMBIES)
HOLIDAY INN (SLEPT 'TIL 7:30pm
Ti Sushi (TIGER BEERS

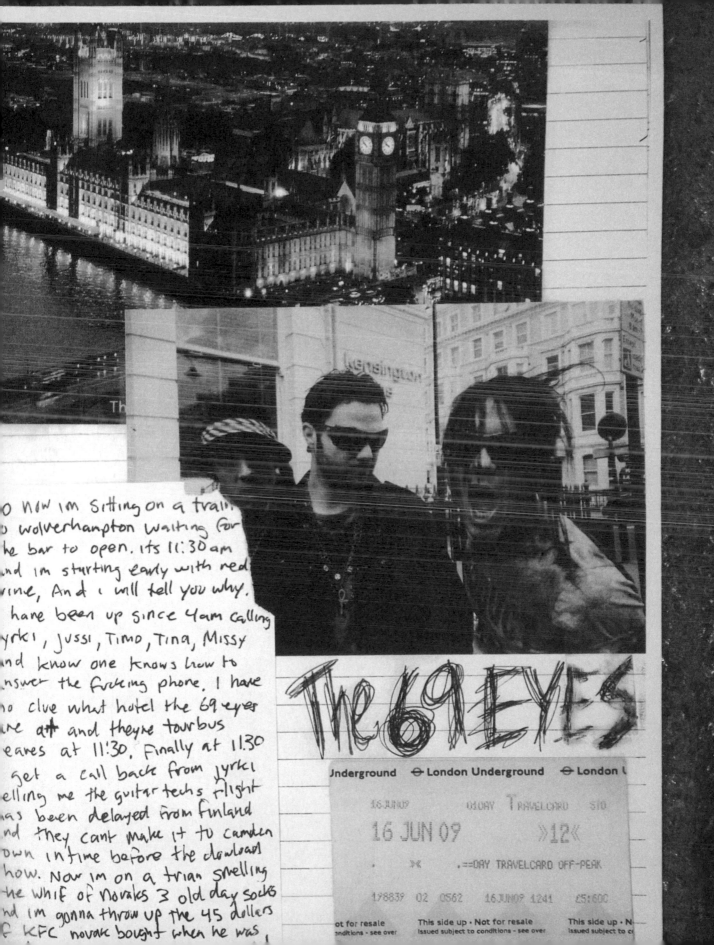

o now im sitting on a train
o wolverhampton waiting for
he bar to open. its 11:30am
and im starting early with red
vine, And i will tell you why.
I have been up since 4am calling
Jyrki, Jussi, Timo, Tina, Missy
and know one knows how to
answer the fucking phone. I have
no clue what hotel the 69 eyes
are at and theyre tourbus
leaves at 11:30. Finally at 11:30
I get a call back from Jyrki
telling me the guitar techs flight
has been delayed from Finland
and they cant make it to camden
town in time before the download
show. Now im on a trian smelling
the whif of Novaks 3 old day socks
and im gonna throw up the 45 dollers
of KFC Novak bought when he was

**THE 69 EYES**

Underground  ⊖ London Underground  ⊖ London U

16 JUN09        01DAY TRAVELCARD    S10

**16 JUN 09**              »12«

⋇      .==DAY TRAVELCARD OFF-PEAK

178839  02  0562   16JUN09 1241   £5.600

ot for resale     This side up · Not for resale        This side up · N
onditions - see over   Issued subject to conditions - see over   Issued subject to c

Camden hotel logic!, NONE!
So we barge into the hotel and
the doorman insist that we are
not staying there, I say "yes we
are here is my room key and its
room 405." The asshole still doesn't
believe me and threatens to call
the police if we don't leave. Plus
Novak keep chiming in threatening
to call his lawyer and makes
matters worse. I try to head for
the elevator and the dude is
not having it. now we are fighting
over my room key, Fighting!!!
Then another guy from the backroom
doing research on us tells the
guy that its legit and we are
staying there. He gives me my key
Back and I say "fuck you asshole
HA!" then I slam my door and call
Him an asshole once more, HA!

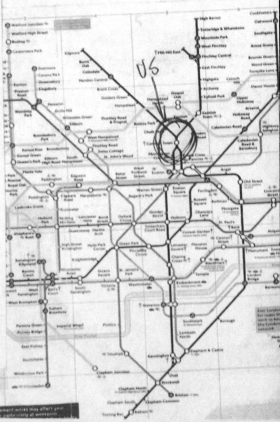

US

8

# CAMDEN TOWN · LONDON '09

"I WANNA BE BAD, I JUST DON'T WANNA
GO TO JAIL — NOWACK"

"I MIGHT JUST GO TO DIE HERE"
— NOWACK

"THERE IS ONLY 7 PEOPLE I'LL
MISS, 1. MOM
          2. LIFE PARTNER
3½ BUCKY — 3 DIVA
          4 & 5. BROTHER & SISTER
          6. MANDY
          7. BILL BUTLER
                    — NOVAK

"BUT THERE'S NOT EVEN
A NUMBER ON THE MAP OF
EXISTING GALAXY FOR DELAWARE
WHORE TO HAVE A SPOT"
                    — NOVAK

"SHE WASN'T AS GOOD AS
THAT TEXAS BITCH
              314-368-1977"

# The 69 Eyes MUSIC VIDEO
## Dead Girls Are Easy - W.C, PA

concept was fun and simple, 4 hot vampire chicks fucking with a nerdy convenient store worker, and they steal him and give him a night out on the town. Sexiest video ever.

BACK IN BLOOD

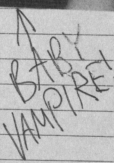

BABY VAMPIRE!

← Caddyshack
Convenient
Store
on RT. 1

After 69 eyes video PA!

I trusted #1 M!!!

7am Right before Jades BAR!

OIDE here, This is the kind of shit that makes you quit drinking!

I didnt mean it, I swear, I mean, maybe, well, it was on purpose!

SIDE > BUM... →

$7 am all night bender with Mankawk, V, olle Jicuso, Frantz (who was a piece of shit) anyway. It was 7 am and we make it to my house and the fine idea comes up to put a glolf ball between oldes ass. Now, I can do it right, or I can do it wrong and make t great. So what do I do? I ack him in the ass as rd as I can and this s what happens ladies and Gentlemen!

FUCK ME!

NOWAK·ME·VILLE

across the street fr[...]
charolette st. hotel wh[...]
I am banned f[...]
pissing in the
basement 7
fucking year
ago. they sti[...]
cant get ou[...]
it. So we ne[...]
across the
street!

Metal Hammer awards—
I am getting ready to present
an award for anvil and
Nowak is blacked out drunk
with his ass hanging out
insisting that a 40 year old
gives up her panties so his
dick and ass wont hang
out anymore. Now I have
to leave with jussi to do
photos and press so I
dont know his condition
when I get back. Now
hes on a search for
coke at the steel panther
[...]party and I insist[...]

That he does not do
it because its 3am and
the night is officially
over! plus we are meet-
ing Ville at noon amoro
in soho, So what does
he do? a fat rail at
3:30 am and i tell him to
Fuck off and roam the
streets of london and
tie! He shows up at 5am
banging on the door and
falls asleep instantly snoring
which drives me nuts.
Because i was almost asleep
now i have to listen to this?

So now i turn on the
tv to drown out the
sound, then i hear a new
noise, its him jacking
off! uhhhh, what a
scumbag, I should have
just knocked his lights out
and put it to an end!

Zille Zalo
00358400759

HAMMER
GOLDEN GODS
TO THE
GOLDEN GODS 2009

FEATURING LIVE PERFORMANCES FROM

TRIVIUM
ANVIL
COMPERE
JASON
ROUSE
AMON AMARTH
DevilDriver
SAXON

METAL HAMMER
GOLDEN GODS
2009
MONDAY JUNE 15
DOORS 6PM, LAST ENTRY 6.45PM

indigo₂ at The O₂

NORTH GREENWICH,
LONDON

VIP TRANSPORT
BOAT LEAVES FROM TEMPLE PIER AT 4.30 SHARP

# Red WINE diaries of November

Freddie Mercury and Novak on the tube to Tottenham court rd! He frenched his 3 sided dick duster as he was reading gay shit!

So Novak shows up to cro-bar asking where the fuck pete doherty is, doing that is asking at Landmark where Bam Marson is, they don't like it. its jealous fratboys. But in this case its wasted up rockers who are jealous he is successful and they are not. We did a carbomb with the owner and staff and made him shut the fuck up!

## The Crobar

Its like a dark hole of fantastic grit and piss. Walls to walll pages of comic's cover god knows what bodily fuids, Music at a volume! ah fuck yeah and dark enough not to realize your about to piss yourself and aint nobody gonna CAR

CROWBAR · SOHO · LONDON 6·12·09

So I'm back at the crowbar, I don't know where the fuck 69 eyes are, and my phone doesn't fucking work here. So I'm 99% fucked. I order 3 red wines and the bartender reminds me how I had to hide upstairs for 3 hours waiting for the cops to dodge me because I jumped off the top of astoria at a HIM show 3 years back and lost my shoe kelly osbourne bet me I wouldn't do it but I did. and the shoe I lost is hung up at this very bar. Not to mention my passport is a missing. So lets rock!

Ville Valo @ fitzroy pub

Wolverhampton TAXI piece of shit who jipped us!!

This fucko took us 2 hours the wrong way plus got stuck in an airshow and traffic jam and we had to get out and piss. I smoked in his cab and said Fuck you. He deserved it!! 1/2

WHAT ENTERANCE WE NEED TO BE AT. WHERE THE FUCK IS THE ARTIST ENTERANCE

# DONNINGTON·ENGLAND '09

Download festival -
So we are now forced to
take a train from camden
to wolverhampton, then
a cab to donnington, well
apparently theirs 2 fucking
donningtons because the
fuckface cab driver took
us 2 hours in the wrong
direction through major
traffic because of an
Airshow. once we get there
Absolutely no festival is
happening. I flip out and
light a smoke in his cab, he
tells me theres no smoking.
I tell him to fuck off

And take me to the nearest train station, the next
train doesnt leave for 2 fucking hours and it's
not even in the right direction. Now I get another
cab 3 hours back to the real Donnington and spend
700 pounds getting there. We get there in the nick
of time for Clutch, 69 eyes, steel panther and
Def Leppard. Novak got jacked off by a floozy
and missed Def Leppard. Then a long drive back to
London with 69 eyes with no beer, Another 300
guid. England is expensive! By the way I introduced
Steel panther to the stage And kicked novak in the
face, half the people thaght I kicked tommy lee because
of novaks belly tattoo. They told me it was fucked up.
BUT ITS NOVAK.!!

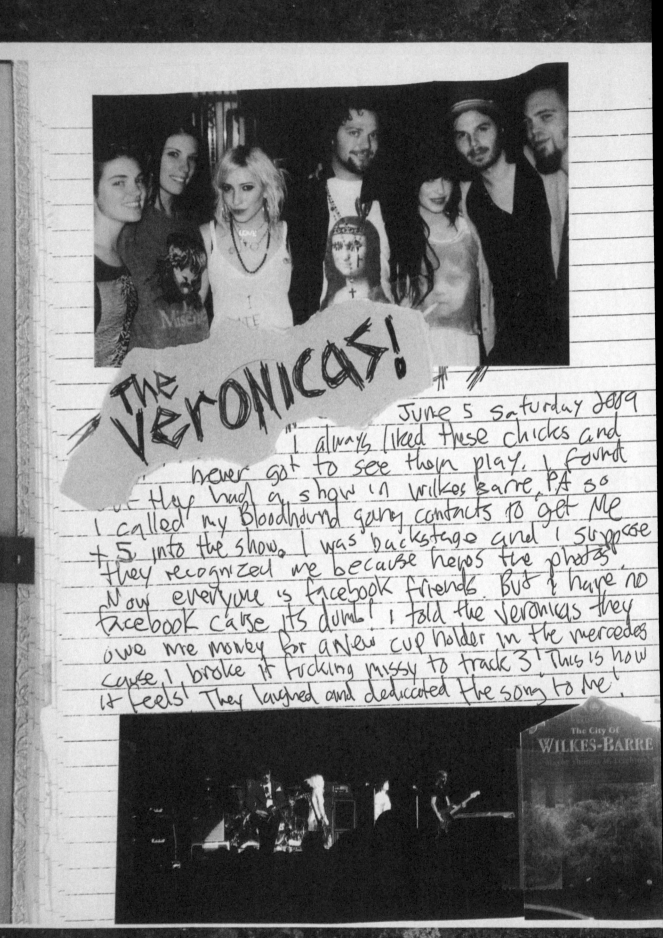

# THE VERONICAS!

June 5 saturday 2009

I always liked these chicks and never got to see them play. I found out they had a show in wilkes barre, PA so I called my Bloodhound gang contacts to get Me + 5 into the show. I was backstage and I suppose they recognized me because heres the photos! Now everyone is facebook friends. But I have no facebook cause its dumb! I told the veronicas they owe me money for a new cup holder in the mercedes cause I broke it fucking missy to track 3! "This is how it feels! They laughed and dedicated the song to me!

The City Of
WILKES-BARRE

# The Agonist

June 6 Sunday 2009

So I meet this band at the note and think its one more night of ordinary bands, but its not! its basically in my eyes cradle of filth with a girl singer with blue hair named Alyssa. I say - rad show, where are you off to and where are you staying? she says "literally in a Walmart parking lot in a van. I say, well thats not happening cause your all coming to my house! they come back and we hop on the quads at 3 am, the dune buggy had a head on collision with a tree $4000 in damages, another day at the house. Well this is them rocking in Allentown, PA. they are from montreal, home of Gorguts!! By the way they can stay at my house whenever they like! I love them!

I was wondering why all these kids in china were wearing shorts with their dick and ass cut out. I thaugh that they all had old ripped clothes and they couldn't afford new ones. Turns out its the new trend out there, if a kid has to shit or piss, it aint gonna be in their pants, it will land on the street, And the parents wont have to clean it up! Good thinkin!!

注意事项

爱护园内古树、古建及文物
注意防火、园内禁止吸烟
珍爱生命、安全出入
遵守园内各项规章制度
每券一人、无副券无效

PHOTOS BY: RYAN GEE, ADAM WALLACAVAGE,
JOE DEVITO, ROGER BAGLEY, MARK WEISS
REDMOWHAWK GEOFF, CLAY PATRICK, JEFF TAYLOR,
BAM AND MISSY MARGERA